HOW TO ACHIEVE BUSINESS SUCCESS IN KOREA

How to Achieve Business Success in Korea

Where Confucius Wears a Three-Piece Suit

Chong Ju Choi

and

Nigel Wright

M

© Chong Ju Choi and Nigel Wright 1994

All rights reserved. No reproduction, copy or transmission of this publication may be made without written permission.

No paragraph of this publication may be reproduced, copied or transmitted save with written permission or in accordance with the provisions of the Copyright, Designs and Patents Act 1988, or under the terms of any licence permitting limited copying issued by the Copyright Licensing Agency, 90 Tottenham Court Road, London W1P 9HE.

Any person who does any unauthorised act in relation to this publication may be liable to criminal prosecution and civil claims for damages.

First published 1994 by
THE MACMILLAN PRESS LTD
Houndmills, Basingstoke, Hampshire RG21 2XS
and London
Companies and representatives
throughout the world

ISBN 0-333-60642-6

A catalogue record for this book is available from the British Library.

Printed in Great Britain
by Ipswich Book Co. Ltd
Ipswich, Suffolk

Contents

Preface	ix
Acknowledgements	xi

1 Land of the Morning Calm — 1
First impressions	1
Stage show for the world	3
Why so special?	4
Challenge for business and family	7

2 A Land Called Koryo — 9
In the beginning	9
Unification	11
Kingdom of the Choson	14
Appearance of Westerners	16
Japanese colonial rule	18
Jubilation turns to division	19
The Korean War	21
Aftermath – towards democracy	23
A 1990s transformation?	26

3 Korean Economic Development — 29
Spectacular growth	29
Exports and government incentives	30
Government strategy objectives	33
Cause of success	36
Changing strategy for the 1990s	37

4 Nature of the Korean People — 39
Origins	39
Primary influences	40
Confucianism	41
Family ceremonies	43
Names	45

	Etiquette and *Kibun*	46
	'Face'	47
	Korean lifestyle and role of women	48
	Korean food	50
	Ginseng	52
	National Dress – *Hanbok*	53
5	**Management Style**	**55**
	Traditions in Korean business	55
	Comparisons in East Asia	58
	Analogies between Europe and Asia	60
	Korea, China and ASEAN	62
	Korea's *Chaebol*	63
	The *Chaebol*'s future	65
6	**Business Etiquette**	**67**
	Truly Korean	67
	Elements of etiquette	69
	Communication	75
	Negotiation	77
	Understand the Korean viewpoint	79
7	**Working with Koreans**	**81**
	Crossing cultural boundaries	81
	Status inside the company	82
	Working hours	84
	Productivity	85
	Confidentiality	85
	Making decisions	86
	Getting paid	87
	Korean education and its results	88
	Staff recruitment	89
	Staff dismissal	90
	Female employees	91
	Unions	92
	Korean executives	93
	Motivating staff	95
	Korean executives representing foreign firms	98

Contents　vii

8　Into Partnership　**101**
　Skin-deep adversity　101
　Courtship and marriage　102
　Conflict sources　104
　Conflict prevention　107
　Conflict resolution　109

9　Enjoying Leisure　**115**
　Discovering Korea　115
　Seoul　117
　Seoul outings　126
　Eastern Korean　129
　Central Korea　130
　South East Korea　130
　South West Korea　132
　Cheju – Island of the Gods　132
　Royal Asiatic Society　134

10　Korean Fact File　**135**
　Constitution and government　135
　Population　136
　Entry points　136
　Communication　136
　Seoul – the head office　137
　Entry requirements　137
　Housing　138
　Schools　138
　Currency　138
　Health care　139
　Newspapers　139
　Language　140
　Hotels and *Yogwans*　140
　Investment in Korea　141
　Types of business operations　141
　Licensing　142
　Intellectual property　143
　Sport　143
　Common abbreviations　145

National holidays 146
The Korean flag 149
National flower 149
Craft and culture 150
Intangible cultural assets 151
Services 152
Useful addresses 153
Suggested reading 154

11 Survival Guide 157
Country sketch 158
Factors affecting economic development 159
Distinctly Korean 161
Character of the people 162
Business culture 164
In a Korean company 166
Conflict 167
Living in Korea 168

Index 171

Preface

Korea is a rapidly changing country, having moved from utter devastation at the end of the Korean War in 1953, to becoming one of the fastest developing countries in the world over the last four decades. It is now the fifteenth largest economy in the world, and the world's tenth largest trading nation. Not only has the global image of the nation been changed; there has also been a transformation in the people's standard of living, and an exposure to a Western lifestyle and a new high technology work environment.

The rapid economic growth has been export-led and Korea has emerged as a key Northeast Asian country, geographically, as well as economically. As Asia's second largest economy, it is a major player on the Pacific Rim and its trading horizons have steadily widened, stretching beyond Japan and the USA towards the European Community and Eastern Europe.

This explosion of activity, often dubbed the Korean 'economic miracle', has attracted much inward investment and technology transfer from around the world. However, foreigners arriving in the modern, bustling city of Seoul have discovered that achieving successful business ventures in Korea depends largely on an ability to cope with the local culture. This is a culture which emanates from deep-seated traditions and a complex history, involving different religious beliefs, domination by other nations and strict adherence to the principles of Confucianism.

This book aims to give foreign visitors an insight into the way Koreans conduct business, and introduce them to some of the delights of a fascinating and dynamic country. It seeks to describe briefly Korea's historical, cultural and economic background and to explain that a basic understanding of the people and their customs can have a profound influence on the success of a business deal, venture or working partnership.

The chapters of the book express the personal views of the co-authors. These have been developed and enhanced over a number of years by interaction between Koreans and Europeans who have experienced the challenges and pleasures of working together. We hope the suggestions and ideas contained within the book can make a meaningful contribution towards any future business ventures with this unique and major Asian country.

CHONG JU CHOI
NIGEL WRIGHT

Acknowledgements

Chong Ju Choi

I would like to thank, in general, the numerous executives, European and Asian, with whom I have spoken to over the years on the topic of European–Asian business, and especially on business in Korea. Many of the ideas in this book were used at various conferences and executive programmes in places such as INSEAD, Harvard University, Henley Management College, Ashridge, Cranfield, Durham University, Birmingham, CBI. Special thanks go to Jin Park, Seong-Deog Yi, Donghoon Oh, and Soo-Hee Lee who have spent a substantial amount of the time with me over the last several years discussing Korean topics. I would also like to thank Templeton College, Oxford, and especially the Dean, John McGee, for providing the ideal environment for carrying out much of the research necessary for writing this book, and to Ms Louise Copeland and Ms Lindsey Farnes for their invaluable patience and help towards editing and proof-reading.

Nigel Wright

Many thanks to my wife, Sue and son, Jonathan for their patience whilst the text of this book was being written and their tremendous support when we lived in Korea. Thanks also to the staff at the Centre for International Briefing at Farnham Castle for use of their resources and for providing me with the opportunity to give presentations on working and living in Korea to businessmen and women about to embark upon such an adventure. I am also grateful to Ron and Sandy Emmitt for giving their time in proof-reading many chapters in the book, and finally my sincere thanks to the many Koreans with whom I have worked and communicated with over the last eight years. Their cheerful disposition, patience and willingness to work long hours to meet objectives has been hugely appreciated.

1
Land of the Morning Calm

In the golden age of Asia
Korea was one of its lamp bearers
And that lamp is waiting to be lighted once again
For the illumination in the East

Rabinchranath Tagore

FIRST IMPRESSIONS

So this is the 'Land of the Morning Calm'? This thought slipped through my mind as I sat in a large black saloon car which had just burned rubber screeching to a halt in front of a Zebra crossing on the road from Kimpo Airport to the centre of Seoul. It was the evening rush hour and it seemed as if the City's entire population was hurtling across this one Zebra crossing, urged on by two policemen each wildly blowing football whistles. Amongst the jostling crowd were businessmen clad in three-piece suits, girls smartly dressed in the latest fashions, elderly ladies wearing what looked like some sort of national costume, a man with a wooden frame on his back, countless bicycles and weaving through the middle of it all, a motorbike with a huge refrigerator strapped above its rear wheel. What a mixture, this country was clearly going to be very different!

I was already puzzled from my very first impressions at the airport. My Korean colleagues who had met my incoming flight had been wonderfully courteous and polite, but why had they insisted I sat on the right hand side in the rear of the car? Why had they already given me a pack of my business cards? Why was a business dinner already being organised for the following evening? Surely they were going to give me a chance to sleep off some of my jet-lag?

Our journey continued towards the city centre and I had quickly decided that Koreans must be a gregarious fun-loving race. There were smiling faces all around and I was soon to learn that they are sometimes regarded as being the Irish of the Orient. And what of religion? I'd been told that Korea was largely a Buddhist country, but as dusk fell across Seoul, dozens of neon red crosses were lit up on churches, and hovered ethereally above the houses on the surrounding hillsides. There was obviously room here for other religions as well, and I was later to discover that apart from the Philippines, Korea is the most Christian country in Asia.

Our car turned and crossed the wide open spaces of Yoido island straddling two channels of the River Han. A backdrop of rocky mountains was silhouetted against a flaming sky beyond the Northern part of the city and my Korean colleague explained they were very popular for hiking and climbing. (I hadn't thought of Korea having mountains never mind being mountaineers!) On my right now was a row of tanks and aeroplanes, a grim reminder of the Korean war and soon afterwards we passed the picturesque old city gate – Namdaemun – at the entrance to an enormous street market.

So by the time we had reached my hotel, I was becoming convinced that Korea was to be a fascinating country in which to live and work. These first brief impressions were both confusing and vivid. Life appeared vibrant, hectic and chaotic. Although there were building sites spawning every conceivable new concrete structure, traditional Korean houses were very much in evidence, often huddled at the foot of high-rise office blocks. Stalls selling all types of vegetables and produce were on almost every street corner. What an exciting mix of a traditional way of life competing against the gloss and invading material wealth of the late twentieth century. There were to be plenty more surprises!

STAGE SHOW FOR THE WORLD

Nearly a year later and so much wiser, we were sitting in Seoul's superb Olympic Stadium for the 1986 Asian Games Opening Ceremony. There was a capacity crowd, expectation was high and security on entry had been rigorous, at least in part due to the recent alleged North Korean bomb attack outside Kimpo Airport. We were very wet. The rain poured down but did not dampen the ardour of enthusiastic Koreans or harm the spectacular display of synchronised Taekwando martial art. The atmosphere crackled with emotion, for this was the dress rehearsal for the 1988 Olympiad.

We had not been disappointed by our first impressions and by now were realising that living and working in Korea was far more intense than in England, or anywhere else we had experienced for that matter! The results of the South Korean nation's positive orientation to succeed were in view all around. Here was a country which had been utterly destroyed by war just thirty years previously, now with a fast maturing infrastructure, and successfully preparing to act as host for the rest of the world. Office blocks and new international hotels were seemingly being opened every week and the banks of the River Han, which winds through the very heart of Seoul, were progressively being bulldozed and groomed into riverside parks and leisure facilities. A second air terminal was under construction at Kimpo and the people themselves bustled with enthusiasm and considerable confidence that the many new projects would be completed in time for the expected massive influx of visitors in 1988.

The faces around us in the stadium that day displayed some of the inner feelings and emotions which pervaded Korea at the time. The immense pride of what had been achieved produced tears from many Koreans. In front of them, the Taekwondo display had given way to a noisy pageant of ethnic music and dancing. Undeterred by the heavy rain, the performers looked dazzling in *Hanbok* – their brightly coloured national costume. Some of the older faces in the crowd showed a puzzled, perhaps even bemused expression. These were Koreans who had not only experienced the horror of the 1950–3 war and its immediate aftermath, but had also suffered under the Japanese control of the country during the first half of the twentieth century. This occupation was a brutal regime aimed at Japanising the Koreans by denying them their language and much of their culture.

Such older Koreans still fear domination from outside and worry that Westernisation – as represented by luxury department stores in downtown Seoul and American pop music blaring from night clubs and discos – is yet another challenge to their sovereignty. They also have a real fear that too much social change, imposed too quickly, will place intolerable stress upon traditional family values. Their values have come from a deep-seated culture largely based on the precepts of Confucianism.

We discovered that despite being driven by economic urgency and desire for worldwide recognition, Koreans often ascribe more importance to manner rather than matter.

WHY SO SPECIAL?

Korea has a unique heritage. After China, Korea has one of the longest histories as an independent nation in the world. Its independence reaches back to AD 668 when the Silla Kingdom achieved unification by defeating two rivals – the Paekche and Koguryo kingdoms. As a result, the Korean people served under one monarch and so started a unified and, sometimes, brilliant culture which continued with only a few interruptions until the twentieth century.

Korea's sense of unity emanates from this feeling of strong independence, but is strengthened by two other important facts. Firstly, Koreans are a homogeneous race, distinct from both Chinese and Japanese. They are thought to be descendants of the wandering nomadic tribes from Mongolia who moved southwards into the peninsula. Secondly, the creation in 1443 of the Korean phonetic alphabet – *Hangul*. This is a combination of twenty four simple symbols which when combined can represent almost any sound, giving the Koreans a significant educational edge over both China and Japan. In fact, to quote H.G. Wells:

> The Japanese writing system remains a clumsy system, though not so clumsy as Chinese. Korea long ago went a step further and developed a true alphabet.

The sense of unity is laid upon deep and unique cultural roots. Together, they make Korea very special. Shamanism and Taoism were the first important concepts to become influential on the peninsula, and this was succeeded by Buddhism arriving geographically through China in the fifth century AD. Hundreds of years of Buddhism followed during which many of Korea's great Buddhist temples were built. By the end of the fourteenth century, however, Confucianism was firmly installed. Confucianism is not a religion but an ethical and social system. There is no worship of a higher being or striving to reach a higher level of existence. It is an all-pervading way of life which aims at the improvement of human conduct and structure and human relationships, incorporating them into a well-ordered social system.

Due to an isolationist policy, Korea became known as the 'Hermit Kingdom', until 1876, when it was forced by Japan to open up its ports for trade with Japan, USA and other countries. The predominantly Confucian philosophy of the Choson Dynasty, led by bureaucrats and scholars, not only encouraged isolationism, but also failed to promote an entrepreneurial desire for change. Korea, therefore, despite her passion for education, lagged behind her neighbours. What little was learned about the West came second-hand via China.

This opening of the doors also introduced Korea to Christianity for the first time. Although most countries in Eastern Asia tend to stick to one particular religion, Korea subscribes to many. In fact, it is allowed for within the Constitution. What makes this even more interesting and significant is that although many Koreans profess to exclusively support one religion, they allow all of the country's spiritual beliefs to influence their daily activities.

The Korean War ended in a truce, which still exists, dividing the peninsula into two separate countries, North and South. This divide had a further great effect upon the unique nature of South Korea. The split at the 38th Parallel left most of the natural mining resources in the North and two thirds of the population in the South. The continuing threat from the North was a considerable incentive to South Koreans to re build their nation. They concentrated their efforts in first catching up and then overtaking the North in economic and particularly military terms. A classic example of South Korea's 'We can do' ethic.

This ethic is just one facet of the nature of the Korean people themselves. In fact, those who land in Seoul after visits to Hong Kong, Taipei or Tokyo, often remark upon the warmth and gregariousness of their new hosts. No sign of the inscrutable Oriental here, just cheerful faces, plenty of attention and sometimes a barrage of penetrating questions! If one also notes that Koreans are loyal, courteous, patient, adaptable, stubborn, nationalistic and yearn for strong personal relationships, one can begin to realise that a complex personality lies behind the smiling faces.

In business as in family life, this unique Korean background has led to a formal well-mannered strict code of etiquette, a natural and logical extension of the values handed down through the generations. This etiquette first puzzled us and then fascinated us as we, step by step, came to terms with the 'Korean way'. We made many mistakes, but through the patience and understanding of our Korean colleagues we climbed the learning curve, to grasp the importance of harmonious personal relationships, the problems of concise communication, obedience to authority and the all-pervading 'presence' of Confucius in the business and manufacturing environment.

CHALLENGE FOR BUSINESS AND FAMILY

Probably the biggest single reason for business failure by Western companies in Korea is an inability to fully understand or come to terms with Korea's complex business etiquette, and the paramount importance of the personal relationship. Business deals sometimes fall apart over breakfast meetings in Seoul hotels entirely due to lack of sensitivity and gross impatience on the part of the Western business executive. The lack of preparation and training undertaken by many major companies for staff visiting or actually going to live in Korea, can often lead to foreigners failing to cope with the culture change.

The purpose of this book is to provide background information for visitors to this sometimes bewildering country. Also to give them a rapid insight into the ways Koreans conduct their lives and business and introduce them to some of the delights of the Korean peninsula. It includes a brief historical, cultural and economic overview and also compares the 'Korean way' with other Asian countries and some of those in Europe. The latter is included to give a wider picture, hopefully leading to a greater understanding of potential difficulties involved in the creation of harmonious and successful relationships between Western and Korean partners. The book should also be seen as a true 'Joint Venture' between two co-authors, one a British executive who formerly worked in Korea, and the other a Korean who has been an academic and living at Oxford University since 1986. We have worked together to try and express our views as a rounded and balanced view of the subject.

A positive attitude whether it be by a short-term visitor or long-term expatriate, together with patience, careful preparation and a willingness to improvise and adjust, will make any stay in Korea more productive and enjoyable. The experience can be exciting, stimulating and pleasant as well as a challenge for all the family, to work in a country that by 1993, was the world's fifteenth largest economy, and the world's tenth largest trading nation. We hope to help you to prepare for the adventures ahead. It is intended to be read well in advance of any visit so additional research can be undertaken. However, if time is short, it is brief enough to be read during the flight to Seoul. A chance to prepare for the country 'Where Confucius wears a Three-Piece Suit'!

2
A Land Called Koryo

Swallows are able to reach the far distant south in spite of their minute size.

Korean proverb

IN THE BEGINNING

The Korean peninsula extends southwards from Manchuria and the easternmost part of Siberia in a southerly direction towards Japan. The Yellow Sea separates Korea from China to the west and the Eastern Sea from the Japanese islands to the east. This geopolitical position at a key crossroads in North Eastern Asia has meant a turbulent past and many attempts at outside influence by other countries. Korean culture and society resembles that of China in many ways, and some of the most important aspects have, in turn, been transmitted onwards to Japan. However, throughout their history, Koreans have been dogged and successful in preserving their own distinct cultural and political identity.

In common with many other countries, the beginning of Korean history lies in folklore and legend. It is said that long ago a wise and brave Heavenly Prince wished to descend from heaven and live amongst men. His father, the Divine Creator, granted the wish and the Prince descended to earth with three thousand followers, proclaimed himself king and governed the universe. One day, he heard the prayers of a she-bear and a tigress who wished to take human form. He took pity on them and gave each twenty pieces of garlic and a bunch of mugwort, saying 'if you eat this holy food and hide yourself in darkness for one hundred days, you will become human'. So the bear and the tiger ate the food and hid in a cave. The restless tiger could not endure the boredom and ran off to go hunting, but the patient bear was rewarded and emerged as a beautiful woman.

The first wish of this bear-woman was to have a son. The Heavenly Prince heard her prayers, made her his queen and before long she gave birth to a son, given the name Tangun, who became the first human king. Tangun established his residence at Pyongyang and is said to have given the name Choson to his kingdom. He ruled with wisdom for over a thousand years before flying back up to heaven and becoming a mountain god. To this day, on National Foundation Day (October 3), thousands of Koreans make the pilgrimage to the summit of Mani-san on Kanghwa Island. Here at dawn they pay their respects and honour Tangun at an altar said to be built by him over four thousand years ago in honour of his grandfather, the Heavenly King. The climb to the summit of Mani-san comes highly recommended for visitors to Korea. As well as a chance to savour some of the land's early history, the countryside is beautiful and the views memorable (see Chapter 9).

Enchanting though the story might be, archeological evidence points towards much earlier life on the peninsula, dating back some thirty thousand years. It indicates a clan structure whereby groups of families were organised by village or blood relationship. It was the basis for a Korean society which still exists today – traditions which ban marriage within the same clan, encourage good relationships between clans and promote exchange of ideas. Shamanism, their religion, was based upon nature – spirits that lived in trees, mountains and rivers and controlled everyday fortunes and events. The Shamans, who were ritual specialists, were supposed to have power over these spirits, held ceremonies on sickness and family matters.

This belief that spirits controlled the forces of nature was not unique to Korea, and was almost universal in primitive man. What is remarkable, is that in Korea it has continued right into the late twentieth century and is still particularly prevalent in rural areas.

UNIFICATION

The Bronze Age arrived in Korea around the eighth century BC and was followed by the introduction of iron. It is thought that the coming of iron tools was instrumental towards the invention of Korea's *Ondol* underfloor heating system. This method involves circulating hot air from a stove through stone-lined flues laid within the floor. Modern Korean houses and apartments still use the same technique although electricity or coal are now the chosen fuels rather than wood.

Just before the third century BC, the first tribal league, Ko-Chosun was supremely powerful. It was centred in what is now North Korea. Other tribal leagues existed throughout the peninsula and power ebbed and flowed until by the first century AD, three kingdoms were emerging to hold the balance. Silla and Paekche in the far south and the much larger Koguryo which reached northward as far as Manchuria. Now, influenced by China, cultural development was stimulated and centralised government was built up around hereditary monarchies. During the centuries which followed, there was considerable strife as the kingdoms fought amongst themselves to achieve territorial expansion. Silla ultimately defeated its two rivals and unified the three kingdoms in 668 AD.

The unified Silla kingdom turned its efforts towards creation of a brilliant culture. Its prosperity and power reached a peak by the middle of the eighth century, by which time the population of the capital, Kyongju, had swelled to over a million people. Amongst the aspects of

Chinese civilization imported in these early years, which included the written language of China, Confucianism, arts and architecture, none was to flourish more splendidly under unified Silla than Buddhism. Believing it would assist state security, Silla's leaders constructed many famous Buddhist temples. These included the beautiful and imposing Pulguksa Temple just outside Kyongju and the wonderful Sokkuram Grotto, one of the oldest surviving monasteries in Korea, immaculately placed on the mountainside above Pulguksa. However, although the influence of the Chinese civilization was significant, it overlaid rather than changed the native culture. Administrative systems were always adapted to suit Korean needs.

Through these early centuries there was a profound 'Korean' influence on Japan as emigrants crossed the sea with both Chinese and Korean advances in technology, art, architecture and culture. Buddhism is thought to have been taken to Japan by an immigrant from Paekche and Koreans fully penetrated Japanese society to the highest levels.

Silla was in decline in the ninth and tenth centuries due to internal rivalries, greed and agitation from the lower ranks of people who were excluded from power. There were many uprisings and eventually Wang Kon, a rebel leader and native of Kaesong, was handed the power of government and he re-united the peninsula choosing his home city as capital. He called his new state Koryo – a contraction of Koguryo – and began a dynasty in 936 AD which was to last over four hundred and fifty years.

Buddhism now enjoyed the protection of the Court and its influence was such that the Buddhist priests gained enormous power. Also under this dynasty, a civil examination based upon a Chinese model, was introduced with the aim of filling senior posts with those educated in Confucian classics and Chinese literature. However, the influence of Confucianism was limited in the Koryo period and Buddhism remained the dominant force.

Both Buddhism and Confucianism relied upon texts for communication and teaching and this led to the development of printing using 'wooden block' technology, later to be superseded by moveable type in 1234 AD over two hundred years before Gutenberg in Europe. A second great achievement of the Koryo dynasty was its outstanding Celadon pottery. Celadon with its characteristic pale green glaze was first imported from the Chinese Sung dynasty. The Koryo craftsmen developed a new technique of inlaid decoration which became the foundation of the superb Celadon which is created today.

Genghis Khan and his Mongol invaders conquered China during the thirteenth century and then overran most of Northern Korea. The ruler of the time, King Kojong, fled from Kaesong to Kanghwa island where he remained isolated and helpless as the Mongols inflicted widespread damage upon most of the rest of Korea. It was during this time that King Kojong had all the Buddhist scriptures, the Tripitaka Koreana, carved upon 81,258 wooden blocks which took sixteen years! These blocks may still be seen today as they are carefully preserved at the Haeinsa Temple. They have been declared a National Treasure and remain the world's oldest and most comprehensive collection of Buddhist scriptures.

The Koryo government remained in a humiliating position, subordinate to the Mongols, for over a hundred years. However, this domination had some important cultural influences. These were due to the transmission of ideas and technology from other races who were also under the influence of the Mongols. Koreans, therefore, gained knowledge of astrology, medicine and even cotton cultivation. In the fourteenth century, Chinese rebellion broke the Mongol regime which culminated in the Ming dynasty. Korean independence was revived and in 1392 General Yi Song-Gye seized power heralding the end of the Koryo dynasty.

KINGDOM OF THE CHOSON

Korea was later to take its name from the Koryo dynasty, but General Yi had swept the past aside and moved the capital to Seoul. He undertook major reforms aimed at reducing the influence of the Buddhist establishment and strengthening the power of central government. He took the throne himself and became the founder of his own dynasty which was to last five hundred years. It was to be the final ruling house of Korea. The new kingdom took as its name the ancient Chinese name for Korea – Choson. The reformers of the time went to great lengths to impose Confucian precepts on Korean life. Rituals which had for years embraced both Buddhist and customary traditions were cast aside. For example, customs in burying the dead, which included cremation were replaced in favour of Confucian ancestor worship and its related ceremonies. This new regime closed temples and reduced Buddhism to an inferior and subservient position. Government by powerful bureaucracy was favoured and the founder of this dynasty was happy to become a figurehead of a leader.

The Yi dynasty's most famous monarch was King Sejong, who came to the throne in 1418. He was a great believer in Confucian-style government and was a meticulous administrator. He also established great centres of learning which undertook studies of politics, geography, medicine, history and the sciences. Fine arts such as porcelain and inlaid lacquer furniture flourished and, on his orders, the lunar calendar was reformed.

King Sejong's finest and most memorable achievement was the invention of the phonetic Korean alphabet, called *Hangul*. It has only twenty-four characters and is reputedly the most logical alphabet in the world. The Koreans have a national day to honour the creation of this precise and unique way of writing. Sejong's own enthusiasm for Confucian-type government allowed even greater involvement by bureaucratic officials, which inevitably led to the demise of royal authority after the end of his reign. Confucianism was rapidly becoming the predominant social system and would prevail into the twentieth century. It was responsible for creating what is now usually called the 'traditional Korean character'.

This greatest of Korea's kings was succeeded by men of lesser ability and the power of the monarchy steadily declined towards the end of the fifteenth century. Trouble from within came from dissenting aristocratic landowners (*Yangban*). External problems materialised in the form of a threat from Japanese invasion. Japan had recently been unified under a supreme warlord, Togotomi Hideyoshi, who had set his eyes upon invasion of China, and to achieve his goal, wanted a route straight through Korea. So, in 1592, he invaded Korea and quickly overran most of the country. Korean fighters on land were no match for Japan's well-equipped army, but at sea a different story emerged. The Korean navy, under the inspired leadership of Admiral Yi Sun-Shin, crushed the Japanese using his now famous 'turtle-ships'. These craft were probably the first ironclad ships in history. Their upper canopies were armoured to prevent penetration by enemy projectiles and boarding by enemy raiders. They had formidable firepower and earned their name from an image of a turtle's head at the bow. It was a victory for technology and Admiral Yi has become a legend in Korean folklore. His statue appears in many public places throughout Korea, most notably in Sejong-no near the City Hall in Seoul.

Undeterred, the Japanese continued their invasion until the death of Hideyoshi in 1598, which brought the war to a finish. The ferocious combat had wreaked havoc upon the Korean population, ruined farming and disrupted the social system. An undying hatred of the Japanese remained. To make matters even worse, the Choson Kingdom was soon under attack from Manchu armies from the North. Battered and bruised, Korea retreated into a policy of isolationism and thus earned itself the nickname of the 'Hermit Kingdom'. Although the isolation was never quite as complete as the nickname implies, Korean contacts with her Chinese and Japanese neighbours were closely regulated. Western influence only reached Korea from China through visiting Jesuit priests. Returning Korean envoys brought back foreign books and maps. One of Korea's earliest Western visitors was Hendrik Hamel in 1653. He was one of the survivors of a Dutch shipwreck and returned to his native Holland after fifteen years, writing a book on his experiences. Although this book provided the first information on Korea, Europeans paid little attention.

APPEARANCE OF WESTERNERS

The nineteenth century was yet another crisis time for Korea. Despite hundreds of years of the Yi dynasty and its occasional brilliance, administration was inefficient and isolationism had made the ultra-conservative ruling classes more and more inward looking. Most of Asia, and Korea in particular, faced the challenge of a technologically superior influence from the West. A small Catholic community had built up, stemming from missionaries who had slipped into the country from China, but Korean officials had declared that Western learning was subversive to Confucian beliefs. Persecution followed and repression of Western teaching deepened with the execution of more Christians and missionaries. In the reign of King Kojong, who came to the throne as a youth, an exclusionist foreign policy won widespread support and in 1866, an American merchant ship, attempting to sail up the Taedong River towards Pyongyang, was sunk with the loss of the entire crew.

Eventually, in 1876, Korea reluctantly opened its ports to Japan. This supposed treaty of friendship followed from a little gunboat diplomacy and resulted in permanent Japanese diplomatic presence in Korea! It was to be another six years though, before the walls of Korea's seclusion policy began tumbling and a treaty was signed with the USA.

This was soon followed by treaties with Austria, France, Germany, Italy and Russia. There was to be no peace for the Koreans, however, as within two years violence flared up again as Japan and China became involved in a power struggle. Both countries were trying to penetrate Korea through commercial influence and the West for the first time actually widened its involvement with the country.

By 1895, the Japanese had swiftly and decisively defeated China in the Sino–Japanese war and China acknowledged Korea's liberation from the old suzerain–vassal relationship. This was no independence for Korea, as a Japanese-sponsored cabinet immediately enacted reforms which included the reorganisation of government, abolition of child marriages, ending of the civil examination system and abolition of class distinction. It was a clear attempt to modernise Korea.

Undaunted, the Koreans who were opposed to the dominant Japanese found a new ally in the Russians. Russian interest in Korea had been apparent for some years but had never been quite so pointed as the Japanese. During 1895, a pro-Russian group associated with Queen Min managed to dismiss the pro-Japanese cabinet. Queen Min was regarded as the real power behind King Kojong's throne and the Japanese minister to Korea quickly organised the murder of the unfortunate Queen.

The balance of power then fluctuated between Russia and Japan and by the turn of the century they agreed an uncomfortable truce. The Russo-Japanese war erupted in 1904 when Japan launched a surprise attack on the Russian fleet at Port Arthur. Korea immediately declared its neutrality, but to no avail, as the Japanese marched straight into the country in large numbers. The sad Korean government had no option but to accept the military intervention and accede to occupation. By the end of the following year control by Japan was fully established and recognised by the Treaty of Portsmouth. Even worse, Westerners thought that Japan's occupation would be beneficial and lift a backward and supposedly corrupt country into a more modern society. Thus there was little interest from the international community when a treaty was signed passing some sovereignty over to Japan. However, the Koreans proved to be troublesome subjects, and the Japanese decided to disband the Korean army. This was hardly a popular move and sparked off waves of rioting. It took many years to curb this stiff Korean resistance which went as far as assassination of the Japanese Residency-General, Ito Hirobumi. Finally, in 1910, one more treaty was enforced, annexing Korea to Japan. Korea's very existence as a separate nation disappeared and the country became a Japanese colony.

JAPANESE COLONIAL RULE

Japan's intent from the beginning was to exploit the Korean economy. Before annexation, Japan had already taken over communications, mining, fishery, timber and the railway. Now began the gradual seizure of agriculture and land ownership. The new central government ruled with a rod of iron and any organised resistance was suppressed by the Japanese army. But the Koreans are stubborn people and on March 1 1919, millions of them took to the streets in a peaceful independence demonstration. The police panicked and the demonstration rapidly turned into a bloody riot. Possibly as many as seven thousand Koreans were killed and many more were injured. Although this 'March First Movement' failed to persuade Japan to grant Korea independence, it did encourage the Japanese to make a few rather superficial changes to their colonial policy and soften their approach – Korean language newspapers were published again, and officials and school teachers ceased to wear swords.

In 1937, Japanese colonial policy moved into a far more sinister phase towards the complete 'Japanisation' of Korea. Japanese language became compulsory in schools and all public places in an attempt to remove the Korean tongue. Korean history was dropped from the education curriculum and the people were ordered to adopt Japanese names. As World War Two approached and the Japanese war with China grew more intensive, hundreds of thousands of Koreans were conscripted to fill the positions left behind by workers who had been drafted into the Japanese army.

Although Japanese rule did indeed bring some material benefits to Korean society, it was not with the local population in mind. The communications infrastructure was related to strategic and defence matters and the earnings from new industries were returned to Japan. Koreans were not trained into key jobs in industry as managers and technical experts were imported from Japan. Korea's colonial period, which ended when Japan surrendered to the Allies in 1945, was a period of terrible suppression and exploitation. The memory lies ingrained in the minds of Korea's older population. It was too bitter an experience to forget.

JUBILATION TURNS TO DIVISION

In 1945, Korea seemed to be free at last to determine its own destiny. The people thought that liberation would mean the restoration of Korea as an independent nation. Jubilation was short-lived being overshadowed by the opposing views of the Soviet Union and the USA. When the Russians entered the Pacific War by attacking the Japanese army in Manchuria, the Americans were gravely concerned that the Red Army would take the whole Korean peninsula. In haste, the USA proposed a demarcation line across the country at the 38th Parallel. The Russians would accept surrender to the North and the Americans to the

South. This demarcation line had the virtue of roughly dividing the peninsula into two halves, and put the capital, Seoul, firmly into the American zone. Both sides accepted the proposal, but that was where similarity in plans and aspirations for the future ended.

The USA saw the demarcation as a temporary expedient on the way to a combined occupation of all Korea. The Russians thought otherwise and their troops rapidly appeared to the North of the parallel. An impasse occurred and the USA turned to the UN in 1947. Meanwhile, the Russians were rapidly establishing a Communist regime in the North under the leadership of their chosen man, Kim Il-Sung. He had been trained in the Red Army and soon gained full control. In the South, the American policy was less far reaching, but acting on the American request, the UN General Assembly called for the creation of a unified government for Korea. The temporary commission which had been appointed to oversee the elections was denied entry into the Northern Zone but went ahead with elections in the South. So, on May 10 1948, just half of Korea chose an assembly to draft a constitution and elect a chairman. This assembly picked Syngman Rhee (Yi Sung-Man) as their chairman and later he became the first President. He was an elderly authoritarian figure who had spent most of his life overseas campaigning for Korean independence. The creation of this separate government in the South prompted the provisional government led by Kim Il-Sung in the North to proclaim itself as the Democratic People's Republic of Korea.

The last Russian troops left the North by the end of 1948 and the Americans reduced their presence in the South to advisory level only. Unfortunately, the USA refused to provide weapons to the South beyond the level of meagre self-defence. The Russians had a different approach and were supplying sufficient arms to Kim Il-Sung's army for it to become a formidable force with a significant superiority in troops and tanks. The scene had been set for the major war which was to start in June 1950.

THE KOREAN WAR

Not only was there a disparity between the armed forces of the two Koreas, but also there was a mistaken belief in the North that the population of South Korea was about to revolt against Rhee's government. Added to this, the Americans had made a statement early in 1950 which announced that Korea was outside the USA's Asian defence perimeter.

The Russians were probably aware of North Korea's preparations for war, but it is believed that they were almost as surprised at the timing of the attack as the rest of the world. Early on Sunday morning on June 25, 1950, huge numbers of North Korean troops poured across the 38th parallel. There was no warning and no declaration of war. Within three days, Seoul had been captured. In Washington, President Truman immediately ordered the US forces into battle and asked the UN to approve his intervention. A resolution was rapidly passed and there was a call to member countries to support the Americans under the flag of the United Nations. Eventually, aid to the cause was given by sixteen other nations who contributed to United Nations Command. Even so, half the troops came from the USA and most of the others were South Koreans. It was also significant that an American general was in command throughout. Initially, this was Douglas MacArthur.

The first two months of the war were a near rout and the North Koreans had pushed the allies back to a small area around the southern city of Pusan. However, in September, a significant counter offensive was launched to break out from the Pusan perimeter and move northwards. The timing coincided with General MacArthur's daring amphibious assault at Inchon on the coast to the west of Seoul. Many regarded MacArthur's plan as foolhardy because of the large tidal range in the Yellow Sea. Reckless it may have seemed to some, but it was very successful. Even now, Koreans talk of 'the day the sun rose in the

West', a reference to the fire of battle illuminating the dawn sky, seen from the mountains around Seoul, as the UN forces blasted their way onshore.

They quickly moved inland to cut North Korea's stretched supply line and the tide of battle turned. By the end of the month, the battlefront had been pushed right back to the 38th parallel. With desire for unification, President Rhee was prepared to go ahead on his own and move further north. MacArthur waited long enough to obtain a new resolution from the UN which authorised the Command to unite the peninsula. By the end of October, the forces were approaching the Yalu River near the North Korean border with Manchuria. Unbeknown to the allied UN force, the Chinese army had already crossed the border, secretly, efficiently and in huge numbers. MacArthur had fatally mistaken the possibility of a Chinese intervention in the war, although the Chinese government had always warned the USA against moving into North Korea. Now the Chinese felt that their own borders were under threat.

The Chinese counter-attack was devastatingly effective against UN forces that were spread out across the widest part of the peninsula, and the intense cold of a Korean winter was approaching. They pushed south and retook Seoul. Through the winter and into the spring and then summer of 1951, the battlefront moved backwards and forwards and eventually reached stalemate just north of the 38th Parallel. This situation encouraged the beginning of a truce negotiation, but the talks dragged on for two long years. At last an armistice agreement was concluded on July 27, 1953. This agreement created a demilitarised zone four kilometres wide stretching from coast to coast. It also created a Military Armistice Commission made up from officers of the opposing armies to administer the terms of the agreement. A Neutral Nations Supervisory Committee containing representatives from Switzerland, Sweden, Czechoslovakia and Poland was set up to monitor the truce. For four decades, this Military Armistice

Commission has met to discuss claims, counterclaims, alleged border violations and more serious incidents, at the border crossing point at Panmunjon.

The cost of war had been dreadful. Total casualties in the North were estimated to be 1–2 million and their cities had been heavily bombed. In the South, Seoul had changed hands four times and industrial production together with the transport infrastructure had been decimated. Millions were homeless and almost 50,000 South Koreans had been killed. Countless more were missing or had been taken prisoner. The UN Command lost nearly 37,000 killed, most of whom were Americans. The war had delivered a potentially fatal blow to any hope of a fast and peaceful reunification of the two Koreas and significantly hardened viewpoints on both sides.

AFTERMATH – TOWARDS DEMOCRACY

The years following the formation of the Republic of Korea in the South found very slow recovery in spite of considerable American aid. Corruption was widespread, resources were badly managed and there was abuse of power. President Rhee's government was authoritarian and personal loyalty, rather than ability, was rewarded. Although Rhee was in danger of being ousted both in 1952 and 1956, he was astute enough to engineer situations which conjured up enough support for him to succeed in re-election. However, by 1960 his Liberal Party had become hugely unpopular due to government corruption, economic stagnation and too much dictatorial rule. Inevitable student demonstrations followed forcing Rhee to promise reforms. He failed and had no option but to resign and depart into exile to Hawaii, where he remained until death in 1965.

The new government was almost the opposite extreme and led by Chang Myon of the former opposition. It was so weak it only lasted a few months before being toppled by military coup. The coup leaders imposed a military dictatorship on the Republic and were led by Major General Park Chung-Hee, a 43-year-old of rural origin. Firm control was established together with a progressive tax system and encouragement for business expansion. To help conserve precious foreign exchange, a programme of austerity was adopted and certain imports to the country were banned. The military government also created the Economic Planning Board and launched the first Five-Year Economic Development Plan in 1962. The following year, pressures to return to civilian government saw Park retire from the army and run as successful Democratic Republican party candidate for the Presidency. Four years later, he won re-election and then secured a constitutional amendment to open a route for him to run for a third term. He succeeded once again, narrowly defeating the New Democratic Party candidate Kim Dae-Jung.

Park's hold on power continued throughout the 1970s as the Constitution was re-scripted yet again. Under this new Constitution, the National Conference, whose membership Park controlled, elected him to a new six-year term as President. His rule finally came to a violent end when he was assassinated in 1979 by the former chief of the Korean Central Intelligence Agency, Kim Jae-Kyu. President Park's own style of democracy was based upon a strong and efficient administration and a series of structured development programmes during the eighteen years he was in power. It served South Korea very well and was the foundation for the country's remarkable economic success in the 1960s and 70s.

Throughout this period, the Democratic People's Republic of Korea in the North was following a different path. Kim Il-Sung, or the 'Great Leader' as he liked to be known, was constructing a self-reliant State integrating characteristics of Korean culture within Communist doctrine. His political skills eliminated any rivals and he aimed to take North Korea away from dependence upon the

Soviet Union and China. His very individual ideology was based upon a personality cult in which he was to be revered by all as the supreme leader and benefactor of the nation. Under this unique regime, economic development was very slow, hampered by state control. Although passion for education was high, the economy could barely provide basic needs and the country has depended heavily on export of raw materials to pay for imported manufactured goods.

Following President Park's assassination, the South Korean government was handed over to Prime Minister Choi Kyu-Itah, who was later named to serve out Park's term. Very soon afterwards, he resigned and was replaced by Chun Doo-Hwan, a two-star general who was named President by the electoral college in 1980. He promised a period of prosperity and national unity but started from a difficult, even chaotic situation.

Chun's accomplishments were significant in that he turned the balance of payments to surplus, exercised important social reforms and engineered peaceful change of administration. Korea arrived on the world map as a significant economic force and preparations were being made to host the Olympic Games. He was, however, plagued with political problems on the legitimacy of Government, and pressure for constitutional change for direct election for President. Korea's Sixth Republic was born out of these issues in 1987 when the middle classes took to the streets, alongside students, to demonstrate for democracy.

Roh Tae-Woo was genuinely first past the post in the Presidential election later that year, and his administration made some outstanding achievements. There was a steady transition from traditional authoritarian government towards a more democratic open style and South Korea opened up ties with the Soviet Union and China. The economy continued to grow and wealth was transferred into the pockets of the Korean domestic consumer. The surprising merger of three of the four major political parties allowed the further progress of democratisation including local self-government in 1991. Finally, despite major acts of terrorism by North Korea during the 1980s – the Rangoon bombing in 1983 and the Korean Air Lines plane destruction in 1987 – Roh's conciliatory policy towards the North encouraged huge progress in dialogue between the two Koreas. They both entered the United Nations as separate countries in September 1991 and at the end of the year signed a joint declaration for a non-Nuclear Korea. With the fall of Communism in Europe and creation of a unified Germany, reunification of the Korean peninsula was a distinct possibility by the end of the century.

A 1990s TRANSFORMATION?

Korea's new President, Kim Young-Sam, who was voted into power in the December 1992 elections, is the first real civilian to win the contest since 1956. In an astonishingly vigorous start to his term of office, the new President is making a headlong attack on the Korean economic and political systems. He has purged the seats of power by removing generals who were considered too close to previous regimes and prised out of office allegedly corrupt politicians. The old fashioned and questionable financial system has also come under attack and he has even won promises from the *Chaebol* to freeze price rises.

Of particular interest to overseas investors is Kim Young-Sam's promise to eliminate many of the infuriating regulations, and open up the economy to foreigners. The aim will be to lower prices and increase competitiveness. Small businesses will be encouraged by a reduction in interest rates and subsidised loans. Hopefully, the deregulation will unclog the bureaucracy in Korea's systems and release funds to revitalise industry. The country's future international competitiveness is at stake and Korea has watched other Far Eastern nations catch up and nibble away at its export markets. Although Kim Young-Sam has popular support for his new sweeping measures, it is a bold gamble. If he can create continuous momentum with his reforms, Korea's democracy will improve and mature, sending positive messages around the world.

3

Korean Economic Development

Gold buys no Experience.

Korean proverb

SPECTACULAR GROWTH

South Korea has enjoyed spectacular growth over the last thirty years, moving from one of the poorest countries in the world in the early 1960s with a per capita income of only $100 to the fifteenth largest economy by 1993 and tenth in terms of total trade. It is arguably the most dynamic economic progress made by any country during the twentieth century and has been achieved by close co-operation between government, business and banking sectors within the country. This astonishing growth rate has changed Korea from a poverty-stricken, war-torn nation based on an agricultural society, to a highly industrial power often heralded as the 'second Japan'. Korean companies are amongst world leaders in such diverse industries as automobiles, semiconductors, chemicals, shipbuilding, textiles, steel and computers. In fact, Korea's largest corporations such as Samsung and Hyundai already rank in the world's top 25 largest companies in terms of sales.

No other country has managed to move so far, so quickly. Although Japan also witnessed phenomenal economic success this century, it had the benefit of an infrastructure upon which to build its growth after the end of the Second World War. Korea, being a suppressed Japanese colony until 1945, enjoyed no such basic luxury. However, the people's indomitable 'we can do' spirit literally drove them forwards from a zero start point, with the country's multinational corporations – the *Chaebol* playing a significant role at the heart of the economic success.

Korea began its export drive, during Park Chung-Hee's presidency, and in 1962 recorded a meagre export total of $55 million. By 1993, exports had shot up to over $100 billion, turning the country into Asia's second largest economy behind Japan. It has become a key business centre, benefitting from its geographical position between China and Japan, and, therefore, potentially provides excellent opportunities for investment by foreign companies. If the present growth rate is maintained, Korea will break into the top ten largest world economies by the year 2000. The way Korea achieved this economic miracle is described in the following overview. Those wishing to enter into a deeper study are advised to read the books by Amsden (1989), Song (1990) or Sakong (1992) which are given in the Reading List in Chapter 10.

EXPORTS AND GOVERNMENT INCENTIVES

In the early 1960s, the Korean Government adopted an export-orientated strategy, making foreign trade a crucial and integral part of domestic economic industrialisation. At the heart of the policies was an incentive system encouraging exports, carefully created institutional arrangements and co-operation between government, business and banking sectors. Because of its limited natural resources – most of the peninsula's natural wealth lies in North Korea – the Government took the decision to look outwards and use exports to fuel domestic development.

The Government intervened in key strategic sectors of the economy. There were three major aspects behind this policy:

- Firstly, it was focused on economic growth rather than on equity or wealth distribution. The Republic was forced to take this stance as it began development from such an incredibly poor beginning after the Korean War. Successful economic growth allowed the government to gain credibility with the population, thereby stabilising the domestic situation within the country.
- Secondly, it was industry rather than services which became the focus of attention. Unlike Singapore or Hong Kong, Korea was not a compact city-state, and so could not develop services as a primary source of wealth. Unlike some of the South East Asian countries such as Malaysia and Indonesia, there were no natural mineral or petroleum-based resources around which to develop an economic strategy. Korea decided, therefore, to allow itself to continuously transform its production from simple labour intensive products to higher technology and more capital intensive areas requiring skilled labour.
- Thirdly, as Korea needed to import all of its raw materials and resources, it had to earn foreign exchange through the export of manufactured products. Outward orientated Korean policy makers became tuned to changes in global economy and the constant need to compete in world markets at accepted international standards.

The simple philosophy behind Korea's economic strategy during this time was the higher and faster it grew, the better. The government produced various five-year plans whereby increased exports had greater priority over other domestic, political and social issues. Export targets were agreed between government and companies and those reaching their goals were provided with various incentives such as government subsidies. This expansionary encouragement led to Korean firms greatly increasing their size. The larger firms then became in a stronger position to take advantage of these incentives and had the capital and technology to allow rapid expansion. They also found it easier to overcome the red tape of bureaucratic administration and government regulations.

To maintain export targets, businesses tended to rely heavily on bank loans. Official interest rates were often close to zero or even negative, which encouraged businessmen to borrow to increase exports. Korea's largest banks were either dependent upon or wholly owned by the government, allowing the control of financial credit as a key part of official policy. This close link between government and banking also led to government control over foreign credit and helped co-operation with business. Successful businessmen were rewarded with medals, and President Park would personally monitor export progress.

This very personal acknowledgement gave the star performers visible social recognition, which further encouraged their drive to reach even better targets.

In 1975, the Ministry of Trade and Industry created 'General Trading Companies' (GTCs) to increase expansion even further. GTC designation required minimum capital of about $2.1 million, annual exports of over $50 million and a certain number of foreign branch offices. The government maintained pressure over them by constantly increasing the minimum export requirement. This led to bankruptcies among unsuccessful companies. In contrast, the government provided various incentives and benefits to the winners, including cash subsidies and preferential bank loans. Korean businesses were expected to maximise exports rather than profits, unlike the accepted norm for Western companies. Profits for these Korean firms became only a secondary objective. The market-place played a much smaller role in business competition and discretionary action by the government was more significant in determining both the creation and results of the leading companies. Competitiveness was also largely determined by the ability to expand exports.

The various policies of Korea's industrial and export strategy are outlined below, and are adapted from Song's book on the Korean economy:

Incentives to Firms

Non-Discretionary	*Discretionary*
Special Tax Measures	Rationing of Domestic Credit
Financial Subsidies and Export Credit	Allocation of Foreign Loans
Low Interest Rates	Decisions concerning Government Subsidies
Tariff Exemptions and Adjustments	
Exchange Control Rates	

Command Procedures

Non-Discretionary	*Discretionary*
Administrative Support in Laws	Government Persuasion
Price and Wage Controls	Allocation of Export Targets
Provision of Infrastructure Facilities	Selective Tax Audits
Tax Inspection	Encouraging Mergers to Increase Efficiency
Export–import Linkages	Co-ordination of Capital Investments

GOVERNMENT STRATEGY OBJECTIVES

The Korean government's economic strategy was based on a series of very successful Five-Year Plans. The first began in 1962 and, by 1991, the sixth had drawn to a close. The objectives of these strategies have varied as the country developed from 'down-and-out' towards its present position as a significant player in world markets. Throughout, the government continued to take an interventionist role in the market, and in some ways, similar to a command type economy. There has been a continuous close relationship between all influential sectors and the country might even be described as operating as 'Korea Inc.' What was different in the Korean approach to market intervention was that it equipped private corporations to strive and increase efficiency in a competitive environment and enter world markets.

1. **First Five Year Plan (1962–6)**
   This first serious attempt to undertake such a comprehensive economic strategy was relatively unorganised, although its major objectives were to increase exports, income and employment. The one aspect that was reasonably well arranged was Korea's trade and export policy. The objective was to increase exports by providing exporting firms with various subsidies, cheap loans and government support and guidance. Rapid expansion of output and exports did occur, but was accompanied by high inflation. Nevertheless, it was a successful first attempt at creating this 'Korean-style' relationship between government–business–banking.

2. **Second Five Year Plan (1967–71)**
   The objectives of the second plan were to help lower inflation generated by the rapid growth policies of the first and to stabilise the overall economy so that it could experience continuous economic growth. Various reforms were carried out on exchange rates, imports–exports, trade and government expenditure. The net result was a rapid growth of both exports and Korea's general economy.

3. **Third Five Year Plan (1972–6)**
   The focus now moved towards development of the heavy engineering and chemical industries, which were seen as 'strategic' and in which the government would help allocate the nation's resources. These industries

were provided with low tax rates, special depreciation allowances and government development help. During this period, domestic savings were not as high as predicted and Korea began to borrow heavily from abroad. This resulted in a crucial foreign debt situation which was exacerbated in 1973 by the first oil crisis. The economy became further destabilised and the inflation rate reached over 40 per cent in 1974.

4. **Fourth Five Year Plan (1977–81)**
   Economic stability was the primary concern of this fourth plan given the instability caused by those first oil shocks. The money supply was fixed which helped stabilise prices. Trade and export policy objectives were to further expand export subsidies and foreign loans to those firms involved in export business. There was also indirect government support to research and development, and training of workers. The 'General Trading Company' concept was introduced at this time, which provided additional incentives to those involved in overseas trade.

5. **Fifth Five Year Plan (1982–86)**
   The 1980s arrived and saw Korea enjoy newly industrialised country status (NIC) along with Taiwan, Hong Kong and Singapore. This prompted the nickname the 'Dragons' to describe these four nations following Japan towards economic prosperity. During this fifth plan, the economy slowed somewhat with increasing foreign debt and high inflation. The government placed an even greater priority on export promotion, diversifying into new overseas markets. The management of the growing foreign debt became a significant new priority for the government.

6. **Sixth Five Year Plan (1987–91)**
   By now, the Korean economy had recovered and was realising high economic growth, low inflation and, for the first time, a trade surplus. Following the successful

hosting of the Olympic Games in Seoul in 1988, the country and people were in confident mood. The government started taking steps towards liberalising the economy and letting market forces play a greater role in domestic industrial competition. Major policies included reducing some government subsidies, privatisation of public enterprises, reduction of foreign borrowing and a general lessening of governmental rules and regulations.

CAUSES OF SUCCESS

There has been considerable debate on the causes of Korea's economic miracle, the players who took part, the role of government and whether this same success could be replicated in other developing nations. The visible hand of government has always been evident and the economy has always been given top priority by Presidents and the various government decision-makers. Relative to Japan, the influence of Korean politicians and their political parties has been minor. Throughout the 1960s and 70s, economic decision-making was authoritarian with the President making key decisions aided and abetted by a handful of advisors and bureaucrats.

The Economic Planning Board was established in 1961 to help oversee the country's economic policies. It was created through a combination of parts of the Ministries of Finance, Home Affairs and Reconstruction. With significant support from the President, the Economic Planning Board allowed certain 'decision-makers' to participate in the plans and controlled critical decisions throughout their implementation. Unlike many other countries, the major strength of the Korean economic policies was in the effectiveness of their implementation. The absolute priority given to trade and export matters was evidenced by monthly meetings attended by the President, economic ministers, senior executives from major companies and a selection of academic economists. The outward-looking strategy was strengthened as the decision makers actively sought the advice of foreign experts. There was a concerted effort to learn from the experience of other countries and international organisations such as the World Bank.

Successful implementation of Korea's economic strategy was carried out using both incentives and disincentives. The government had the discretion to create incentives such as tax subsidies and loans, and if firms failed to comply with 'directives', a number of disincentives were brought into operation, such as tax audits, suspension of bank credit, or recalling of company loans. The 'discretionary' rules that dominated the previous two decades began to change in the 1980s as policy-makers moved towards reliance upon non-discretionary measures and market forces. However, the excellent co-operation between government, business and banking continued to flourish.

CHANGING STRATEGY FOR THE 1990s

The 1990s and the early years of the twenty-first century will provide many challenges to Korea's extremely successful economic policies. However, several major issues will have to be addressed by their strategists, because Korea is now a significant worldwide trading nation, not just an influential economic powerhouse in Asia.

Firstly, the internal Korean market will need to be fully opened up to foreign products and inward investment. Such an opening, together with full liberalisation and increased real competition from foreign sources, will have a substantial effect upon domestic economic policy. This liberalisation was begun in the 1980s and is expected to be completed in the present decade. It is likely to include everything from imported finished goods to increased foreign participation in Korea's developing stock market.

Secondly, there is an urgent need for Korean industry and its research institutes to begin innovative research work and develop new products and processes. Up until now, Korea has depended mostly on American, European and Japanese transferred technology, imported through various licensing agreements. In order to take the step towards becoming a fully developed country, Korea must invest significantly in both the quality and quantity of its original research projects.

Thirdly, Korean economic policy will need to adopt a far more 'international' approach to world markets. Traditionally, Korea has depended upon two countries for the bulk of its trade – Japan for imports and the USA for exports. The country not only needs to address this chronic imbalance, but also develop much stronger relationships with the countries of the European Community.

Some of Korea's protective policies implemented during its developmental phases of the last forty years will be regarded as unacceptable in the intense global competition predicted during the next decade. World class quality at a fair price will become an accepted standard. However, the 'we can do' spirit of the Korean nation has risen successfully to many challenges in the past, and the rest of the world would do well to note that the expectations of these resolute people may be realised yet again.

4
Nature of the Korean People

When you see a worthy person, endeavour to emulate him. When you see a unworthy person, then examine your inner self.

Confucius

ORIGINS

To begin to understand the Korean way of life and overcome the initial culture shock of conducting business, touring or living in Korea, it is important to grasp the people's background and history. Many aspects and consequences of their history come together to build the characteristic qualities of the modern Korean. Their origins are shrouded in the mists of time but ethnically they belong to the Mongolian race and are descended from several Mongol tribal groups who migrated from what are now Siberia and Manchuria. Study of the language and the archaeology of the splendid Silla kingdom, particularly the crown jewels, points their origin to the Altaic civilization which once flourished in Northern Asia. Although their centre lay in the Ural-Altaic Mountains, the Altaic tribes were mobile and gave rise to a whole family of languages from Finland, Turkey and Hungary all the way across Siberia to Mongolia, Manchuria and Korea. The unique Korean tongue, which bears no relationship to Chinese, is perhaps the earliest element of the many factors which contribute towards the national unity and individuality of the Korean people. Very early in their history, they had become fused into a homogeneous race, independent from their neighbours and Koreans have shown remarkable resilience over thousands of years in maintaining and building their own identity despite invasions and occupations from nearby countries.

PRIMARY INFLUENCES

Because Korean cities and shops have a glitzy Western façade, the uninitiated visitor can fall into the trap of assuming that the personality and character of the Koreans themselves have also been internationalised. This may be true for a few who have worked and studied abroad, but the vast majority of Koreans still carry the traditions of their ancient culture, the primary influences which make up their way of life. They are fiercely nationalistic and greatly appreciative of their own country, their cuisine, the beauty of their women, their art and literature, the skills of their craftsmen and the magnificence of their mountain scenery. Koreans are courteous and loyal, but handled unwisely can become a lifelong enemy. They are attributed with great patience, can be extremely stubborn but also very adaptable in their everyday life.

Korean **stubbornness** probably dates back to the Taoist religion of their early history. Taoism concerns itself with harmonisation of man with nature and suggests that water is the strongest of all the elements – an element which is capable of wearing away even the hardest of rock over a long period of time. Taoist principles also embody contentment, longevity and **patience**.

Buddhism, which came to Korea from China during the Three Kingdoms period, also encouraged patience by its philosophical view that salvation in afterlife can be attained by personal effort and conduct throughout life on earth – a slow and evolving process to achieve the essential nature of Oneness in ourselves. Confucianism, despite being an outwardly rigid system to improve human conduct and structure all human relationships, actually developed into a much more pragmatic philosophy over time. It encouraged **adaptability** as a way of pursuing and then achieving political and practical advantage. Something at which the Koreans are most adroit in business today.

CONFUCIANISM

Although much of the Korean character emanates from the early history and religions, the basic conduct of Koreans is unquestionably founded in the principles of Confucianism (*Yu-gyo*). It has been the paramount influence for the last five hundred years and any successful relationship with Koreans must, therefore, be founded on Confucian principles.

Confucianism is an ethical and social system, not a religion as such. There is no worship of a higher being or striving to reach a higher level of existence. It developed as an all-pervading way of life which attempted to improve human conduct and structure all human relationships into an orderly social form. The main traditional requirements were:

- Absolute loyalty to the hierarchy within the structure of authority, be it family, community, organisation or nation.

- Trust between friends and working colleagues. This was deemed to be an important virtue.

- Allegiance and respect to parents, incorporating love and gratitude.

- An orderly and clearly defined conduct between children and adults. All children were taught to be deferent to their parents and grandparents. They spoke only when spoken to, bowed when expected and only used respectful language.

- Separation of husband and wife. They conducted their lives almost in total exclusion from one another. Men conducted their business affairs and women were responsible for running family matters. Even as late as the first part of the twentieth century, some women in Seoul were only allowed out of their houses in the evening to chat and socialise with each other.

Although the physical separation of husband and wife may not now seem quite so apparent, these Confucian principles are still very much alive and flourishing in Korea today. Harmony and trust in personal and business relationships is a dominating force. The establishment of order and placement of individuals within a clearly defined hierarchy is critical to confirm both status and authority. There are five hierarchical relationships:

> Subject obeys ruler
> Son obeys father
> Wife obeys husband
> Younger brother obeys older brother
> Younger friend obeys older friend

The importance of conduct within the ranking of the social system can now be seen. There is also a basic desire for peace and order in a laid down and controlled environment. Respect for ancestors, grandparents and elders remain key elements in creating and demonstrating the right attitude. Relationships, as a result, tend to be vertical with age and position within the hierarchy accentuated by different language forms. There are different ways of speaking dependent on whether talking to superior, parent, friend, child or wife.

Although Confucianism has no organised churches or formal worship, there are many Confucian academies in Korea. Here, ceremonies are held to honour Confucius and other Korean and Chinese scholars. Some involve traditional music and are colourful spectacles. One well worth visiting is the annual event at Chongmyo in Seoul. It gives the visitor a thought-provoking insight into a traditional Confucian ceremony. A wonderful glimpse into the past.

So Confucianism is the most important key to Koreans' distinctive identity and underpins the principles of society and business. It has survived, surprisingly intact, despite the country's long history of domination by other people and internationalism of the late twentieth century. It won't disappear in a hurry, Koreans are resolute people!

FAMILY CEREMONIES

It is impossible to stay long in Korea without coming across or becoming involved in a Korean family ceremony. There are many such rituals and the Chinese actually used to call the Koreans 'the ceremonious people'. Until quite recently, the average life expectancy of a Korean was quite low. Men, in particular, did not normally live much beyond the age of 50, so reaching a sixtieth birthday (*Hwangap*) was regarded as a considerable achievement. At 60, a person has successfully completed 5 twelve year cycles of human life, based on the Chinese Zodiac system. It was, and still is, regarded as a considerable landmark and the point where he or she is supposed to retire from active life, take some rest and assume the mantle of an elder. The occasion is celebrated with major pomp and ceremony. Traditional dress of *Hanbok* is worn, gifts are received and a sumptuous feast is followed by drinking, music, dancing and singing. They are wonderful parties where inhibitions are cast totally aside!

Infant mortality was also high, so much so, that the celebrations for the birth of a child were held on the hundredth day of life. At this point the worst perils of the child's brief existence were over and a big party was thrown for family and friends. Even now, the occasion is celebrated and pictures of such events can be seen in photographic shops in Korean cities, sometimes to the amusement of visitors, who see a child in traditional costume, surrounded by carefully constructed piles of fruit and rice-cake. The baby's first birthday is also celebrated, but after this, it is probably fair to say that birthdays are considered to be of no great merit for another fifty-nine years!

Traditionally, most Korean marriages were arranged, often with the aid of a matchmaker. A girl would marry young and her family would formally carry her trousseau and her own Korean-style storage chest around to the boy's home prior to the big occasion. The groom's family would reciprocate with gifts appropriate to their economic status. On the wedding day, the bride, clad in brightly coloured *Hanbok*, would be carried in a palanquin to the groom's house for the ceremony, and the couple (maybe even meeting for the first time) would pledge their troth over a cup of rice wine.

This ceremony is now only to be seen as a 'Stage Set' for tourists at places like the Korean Folk Village. However, some of the ritual has developed and been transferred to the Wedding Halls in the towns and cities. Often nicknamed 'Wedding Factories', the Halls contain rooms of various sizes and can have many weddings proceeding simultaneously. The unwary foreign visitor can easily find himself in the wrong wedding on a busy Saturday afternoon in Spring! Brides will look somewhat bewildered in their gorgeous, sometimes flamboyant wedding gowns and the grooms very solemn, but resplendent in tuxedos.

A piano or organ will play Mendelssohn's familiar *Wedding March* and small children will run uncontrolled up and down the aisles. None of the peace and serenity of a Western wedding here, but it's great fun and the cameras and video recorders are kept very busy! Honeymoons are often very short, maybe just a weekend in Cheju Island before the groom returns to work and the bride to help look after her parents-in-law. Although some couples can now afford to buy their own apartment, many will live with the groom's parents for the first few years of married life. Guests to Korean weddings bring gifts, usually cash sealed in envelopes, and it is quite normal for them to receive a small gift in return, perhaps a towel and bar of soap.

NAMES

Almost all Koreans have three names and the family name is always placed first. There are more than two hundred Korean family names but over half the population is called Kim, Park or Lee. Min, Oh, Choi, Han, Chung and Shin are also very common. This unusual situation stems from a combination of the ancient Clan structure and Confucian reverence for ancestors. Maintenance of family names was thereby encouraged as a matter of prestige and honour.

The second name is a generation name which is chosen by parents, grandparents or onomancer ('name-chooser'). The given or personal name is placed third. Much effort is put into selection of both names and as the family expands, generational names are continued so eventually even distant relatives can have a common name that can be traced back to an ancestor.

Korean women do not change their names after marriage. Although Westerners may address a lady as Mrs. Park, Koreans will know her either by the maiden name she was given at birth or as the wife of Mr. Park!

To circumvent the difficulty of the fact that so many Koreans are called Kim, Lee or Park, which can cause daunting communication problems for a foreigner working inside a large company, Koreans use titles connected with their rank and profession. So the many Mr. Kims can conveniently be separated into Director Kim, Deputy Manager Kim, Supervisor Kim, etc. This has an added personal touch because to use the title indicates respect for their status and position. Titles serve a very important function because Koreans always want to accurately place the people they meet – a Confucian trait. This allows them to speak correctly, judge the level of respect and help create the right relationship. Foreigners should only call Koreans by their first names if a close personal relationship has been built up over a long period, usually years. So family name and title should almost invariably be used when addressing Korean colleagues in business and social situations.

In addition to the mystifying subtleties of respect shown by Koreans when they meet, which as we have seen depend upon age, position and family precedence, they also bow. A person of junior rank bows lower than the senior. The foreigner living in Korea would do well to take due note of the custom and practise it himself when meeting senior Korean businessmen and government officials. It is courteous, polite and will be received very favourably.

ETIQUETTE AND *KIBUN*

Koreans are a very well-mannered people with strict codes of etiquette. Harmony in their personal relationships is a dominating force in their lives and, like so much else, dates back to their Confucian past. Unlike Westerners, Koreans will go to almost any length to prevent conflict and always avoid appearing rude or impolite. Their behaviour, as a result, can sometimes belie Western logic.

This leads to situations which baffle the apparently common sense view of the occidental mind. To a Korean, it can be far more important to appear to be correct and within the bounds of the rules of etiquette, than to become confused by the inflexibility of pure logic!

Meetings and receptions can be very formal occasions, particularly if high-ranking businessmen or government officials are present. Treatment of Westerners is equally formal and visitors must reciprocate to be courteous. No back-slapping! Experienced businessmen and technical professionals receive especially respectful treatment as they are regarded as 'teachers' who have wisdom and can transfer knowledge and skills.

Korean etiquette also consists of an elaborate series of formal gestures designed to create pleasant feelings, a good mood and harmonious relationships. It is an important part of Korean psychology and is called *Kibun*. Koreans are very sensitive to anything which may damage *Kibun* and will go to great lengths to avoid matters which may harm comfortable feelings. It can, therefore, play a decisive role in business because Koreans do not like to be bearers of bad news. Be prepared for unpleasant information to be withheld until the end of a meeting at the end of the day. In the Korean mind, such news is capable of damaging *Kibun* and putting relationships in jeopardy. In all personal and business dealings, unnecessary attacks on anyone's *Kibun* should be avoided. Creation of good mood and feelings will do much to advance negotiations, business decisions and even service in shops, restaurants and hotels.

'FACE'

Not only do Koreans feel that reporting of bad news should be delayed as long as possible, they also find it extremely hard to admit failure as this loses 'face', a trait in common with many other Asian countries. 'Face' is protected and maintained, sometimes at unbelievable costs to the efficiency of an enterprise. Any threat to face by action or sometimes unintended remark is taken very seriously and can stop business deals, negotiations and plans literally 'stone dead'. The Western way of handling errors, dishonesty and incompetence can be unacceptable to Koreans, particularly if a person's self-respect is in danger.

All who visit, work or live in Korea must constantly tune their personal 'antennae' to potential face-loss situations and circumvent them whenever possible. It is a prominent feature of everyday life in Korea and even junior staff will go to extreme lengths to prevent loss of face of their superiors. The visitor must learn to give the Korean an escape route when face threatens the status quo. He must never reprimand a person in the presence of his subordinates, and always calculate whether or not his own actions are putting a Korean in a position of embarrassment or humiliation. Westerners often provide a rod for their own backs by thoughtless remarks which put Koreans in an intolerable position. They then make the situation even worse by blaming the Koreans for lack of consideration and failure to use Western logic!

KOREAN LIFESTYLE AND THE ROLE OF WOMEN

Traditional Korean homes can still be seen around Seoul though many have been destroyed to make way for construction of large tower blocks of apartments. These one-storey homes were constructed around a square courtyard and contained small rooms whose floors were lined with smooth varnished paper. Under the paper the flooring material was baked clay which contained flues for carrying the heat from the cooking fire. This radiant heat system, called *Ondol*, dates back centuries and was an effective way of keeping out the intense cold of the Korean winter.

Chests for clothing, blankets and books lined the walls of the rooms and silk cushions and low tables encouraged the dwellers to live close to the warmth of the floor. Bedding was unrolled each evening and covered with a silken quilt. Rooms had sliding doors, which were really intricately designed wooden grills covered with translucent rice paper. On entering the house shoes were always removed and exchanged for simple slippers.

A woman's task was to keep the house immaculate and look after her husband's parents. Her activities could be constricting and much of her time would be spent washing, cooking, supervising the children, preparing rites for ancestors, sewing and perhaps developing embroidery skills.

Women were, therefore, entirely subservient within the family and in society. Confucian rules actually resulted in laws which emphasised the inferiority of the fairer sex! They were prohibited from marrying more than once and could be expelled from the household if they failed to produce a son. Women's identity was restricted largely to being a supplement to the male of the species until 1948 when the Republic of Korea was established. Then the principle of equality of the sexes was actually written into the Constitution.

The discrimination against women was taken to extraordinary limits. A widow, who then kept her chastity until the end of her life, was given special recognition, but a woman who re-married was punished by having her progeny barred from respectable society for generations.

Exposure to education, the coming of Korea's industrially- rather than agriculturally-based society, and the influences of the west have done much to improve the lot of Korean women. They now go to university and enter business and professions. However, many are encouraged to give up work after marriage, either by pressure from the family or business itself. Young married couples visit restaurants together and visit homes of friends. An increasing number buy their own apartment thereby gradually reducing the tradition of the new young wife looking after her parents-in-law.

The new Korean woman can wield formidable power within her own home. She often takes the cash on her husband's pay day and then organises the family's finance. In some cases, the husband is then given his allowance for drinking and entertainment. The wife will not only pay the household bills and ensure the children are fed and clothed, she will also handle financial investments for the future. She may join a group of women who club together to invest in property and the stock market in Seoul. In fact it is estimated that a surprisingly large portion of funds invested in Korean stocks and shares come from this source. Formidable power indeed!

KOREAN FOOD

No chapter on the Korean people would be complete with at least a mention of the local cuisine. Hot spicy Korean food attacks the Western palate with a vengeance and usually a visitor's first experience of *Kimchi* is one that is never forgotten. Korean food is as unique as the character of the people and has two important ingredients which can make both mouth and eyes water – garlic and piping hot red peppers.

No Korean meal is served without *Kimchi*, which is a form of pickled cabbage. Taste varies according to the vegetables used, but the principal spicy ingredients are garlic, onion, peppers, and ginger. Housewives pride themselves on the quality of their *Kimchi* and it is even eaten at breakfast time along with their staple food of rice. One of the most important events in the Korean calendar is *Kimjang* in the autumn. The city streets in Seoul become blocked with wagons carrying vegetables in readiness for women to buy huge quantities of cabbage and white radish to prepare the winter stock of *Kimchi*. Once made, this *Kimchi*

Nature of the Korean People

is stored in large earthenware jars which are buried to their necks in the ground. Temperature is all important. Too warm and the *Kimchi* ferments, turning sour. Too cold and it freezes. Throughout the chilly Korean winter, *Kimchi* has been a traditional and important source of vitamin C. In fact, it is said that, in early seafaring days, Korean sailors never suffered from scurvy, a fact attributable to the *Kimchi* stocks which accompanied them on board ship.

Although the importance of *Kimchi* to the Korean cuisine, be it a simple lunch or a sumptuous feast, cannot be underestimated, there is much more to Korean food and there are many tasty dishes which will appeal to the visitor. Possibly pride of place and the most popular with Westerners are *Kalbi* and *Bulgogi*. They are barbecued beef dishes with the strips of meat marinated first in a lightly spiced sauce. The meat smells delicious as it is cooked over red-hot charcoal at the table. On a warm summer night in an open-air restaurant, Korean barbecued beef washed down with the local 'light' beer or smooth *Pop-Ju* rice wine, can be a meal fit for a king.

Maeuntang is another popular dish and is a spicy hot seafood soup made from white fish such as a snapper. Sometimes served with a poached egg, it is ideal on a cold winter's evening.

A dish which attracts the eye as much as the taste buds is *Kujol pan*. It is served on a round plate with eight different foods in compartments shaped like the spokes of a wheel. The foods, which may be carrot, bamboo shoots, beef, cooked egg white, turnip and leafy vegetables, are selected using chopsticks and placed on a light pancake. This is rolled up and is just the right size for a tasty mouthful.

An important part of a Korean meal is the soup. It can be made from all sorts of ingredients including seaweed, pine nuts, anchovies and mixed vegetables. Considering the fiery nature of much of Korean food, some of these soups are very bland and a welcome relief to the Westerner suffering from too much garlic and too many peppers. Spread around the Korean meal table will be all sorts of side dishes of radish, spinach, lettuce, cucumber, sesame leaves and hot sauces. They are carefully prepared and add much to the colour and variety of Korean cuisine. A table well-laid for a Korean dinner is a splendid sight and the hostess will take great pride in providing as much variety as possible. Each diner has a small plate upon which are placed morsels of food deftly chosen from the myriad of dishes using chopsticks. Becoming really involved in a Korean feast is a fascinating culinary experience but the breath will smell strongly of garlic the following day!

The main dish for a Korean at any meal is not the meat or the fish but the rice. This is of the 'sticky' variety rather than the long-grained fluffy type favoured in Europe. Koreans will often eat large quantities at a sitting and smile sympathetically as the visitor struggles to finish his first bowl. As with all other Korean food, the diner should eat as much as he or she wishes. However, it is sometimes better to leave just one item in a dish. Many hostesses will keep replenishing empty dishes until everyone is finished.

GINSENG

Amongst the finest delicacies of a meal at an expensive restaurant is the sliced root of Ginseng. It is eaten after being dipped in honey and the resultant mixture of bitter-sweet taste is a wonderful contrast to the *Kimchi* and peppers. Ginseng – the elixir of life – is Korea's most popular herb and the curer of all ills. It has been used for thousands of years in herbal medicine in North East Asia and grows wild in rural areas of Korea. It is now cultivated as a very successful commercial crop and can be seen growing on Kanghwa Island. The root takes up to six years to mature, and after harvesting, the plants are washed, steamed and dried. Ginseng has become a major export industry for the country and Koreans totally believe in its all-embracing efficacy. Its many reported benefits include increased mental and physical powers, improved digestion and supposedly revitalised libido.

Koreans have not been slow to realise that Ginseng taken in the form of capsules or tablets, soft drinks, alcoholic drinks, sweets and instant tea can potentially boost sales and earn valuable foreign exchange. The result is a multi-million dollar industry and growing popularity of the product worldwide as an alternative medicine, but the nicest way to take it is still as the sliced root with honey!

Korea without Ginseng would be unthinkable.

NATIONAL DRESS – *HANBOK*

Chinese clothing dominated Korea throughout most of its history and it was only in the thirteenth century after the Mongol invasion that the evolution of *Hanbok* began. It started with baggy trousers and puffed-out dresses. The waistline was lifted and the vest was then shortened and tied across the chest with a long ribbon. This short jacket, called *Chogori*, had wide sleeves, and is a name from Mongolian which has remained to the present day. Although fashions have changed and developed, the basic concept of twentieth century *Hanbok* is unchanged.

Silk was the preferred fabric for court and leading government officials. Cotton and hemp were the materials used by all other classes of people. Hemp was the most important and traditional fabric used by the Koreans, with white as the dominant colour. Some visitors to the country actually called the Koreans 'the white-clad people'. Hemp was always worn at time of mourning, but because of its gauze-type weave became very popular for everyday wear. In the hot sticky summer months it allowed the body to breathe freely. Even now these hemp clothes are worn by some of the older people and can be seen in the parks and open spaces in hot weather. The slopes of Namsan Mountain in Seoul are a favourite gathering place for this older generation.

Fashionable modern *Hanbok* is worn by many Koreans for special occasions such as a sixtieth Birthday and on national holidays – particularly those such as *Chusok* which might involve a visit to an ancestor's grave. *Hanbok* is an important part of the Korean identity. It is a unique form of attire. The dazzling primary colours now used in ladies' *Hanbok* are bright, outgoing and intense, much like the Korean people themselves.

5
Management Style

Work done depends on effort, not words alone;
Likewise a person is judged by his heart, not his appearance.

Oriental wisdom

TRADITIONS IN KOREAN BUSINESS

To understand Korean business behaviour, etiquette and the way Korean managers behave, it is important to know something about the values that underpin the business culture. Many of these values can be found in folklore and stories which are told, not only to children, but are also repeated to businessmen in order to create rules and emphasise traditions in a changing business world. The concepts of commitment, seniority and humility are three of the most important:

1. **Commitment**
   In Korean folklore, there is a popular story from China, dating back to the fourteenth Century BC. It concerns General Su, who was preparing for battle, but found he was heavily outnumbered in terms of troops, weapons and supplies. In spite of the overwhelming odds against him, he won the battle against the superior forces of his enemy General Li, by adopting two important actions. The first, similar to a 'burning bridges' tactic, was to place his regiment with its back to a river, so there was no possi-

bility of retreat. The second, and even more important, was that General Su placed himself in the front line, thereby revealing his absolute commitment to battle and willingness to expose himself to the same dangers as his troops.

A more recent tale, from the 1980s, is told about Kim Woo-Choong, founder and Chairman of the Daewoo Corporation, one of Korea's most successful companies. Chairman Kim has never been afraid to work under the same conditions as his staff, and when Daewoo's Shipbuilding Division was facing bankruptcy, he moved his headquarters to the dockyard to live and work with his employees. This personal determination and commitment to save the Division, rather than take the easy decision to sell it off, was the significant factor in its recovery. He is one of the most respected and admired managers in Korea.

The idea of 'burning bridges' is familiar to both Western and East Asian cultures and management practices. Chairman Kim's demonstration that he was prepared to incur the same hardship as his employees is probably more typical of East Asian management and leadership style, and especially in the case of Korea's major conglomerates. It is a style which motivates staff to perform most effectively.

This committed approach to leadership is a major difference of management style between Japanese and Korean corporations. In Korea, great authority can be held by one individual, such as the chairman of the company, and this assists him to make a greater commitment to the task than under the Japanese consensus approach. It is possibly one reason why the Koreans managed to enter high-risk and competitive industries such as semiconductors, automobiles, shipbuilding and chemicals so successfully and in such a short period of time.

2. **Humility**
   One tradition which Korean children are taught, is the importance of being modest and humble, and it is a characteristic that permeates right through Korean business society. Modesty and humility are seen as crucial in human relationships and also a way to subordinate an individual's welfare to a level below that of the group. As a result, it becomes easier for the individual to work within and towards the group's agreed objectives.

   Korean children are told the story of a Duke Chuang who had difficulties governing his district. The wise sage, Master Mu-Sun, used the analogy of comparing fire and water to analyse the Duke's predicament. Although the fire whilst it is burning is seemingly invincible, it does eventually burn out. Whereas water, starting only as a small stream in the mountains, permeates every crack in the land and humbly touches and fills every crevice. So in terms of leadership, Master Mu-Sun explained, it is not always the most thrusting and dynamic managers who succeed, but frequently the humblest of leaders, who are closer to the common people.

3. **Seniority**
   The concept of an old 'wise' man such as Master Mu-Sun is very common throughout Korean culture and tradition. It is graphically shown today in Korea, by society's respect for the elderly and aged. Because of the importance of the family, the traditional structure has been enlarged and embraces three generations – grandparents, parents and children. Although reverence for the grandparents in the extended family structure has declined in recent years, it still remains one of the mainstays of Confucian beliefs.

   This respect for seniority is very visible in Korean

companies and encourages the authoritarian management culture so prevalent throughout all forms of business. Respect for elders is shown by subservient behaviour in the presence of the older and most senior staff and includes a deferent form of address used in conversation.

COMPARISONS IN EAST ASIA

Although classic children's stories referred to ancient political and military rulers, many of the fundamental traditions have remained influential in Asian management styles. A better understanding of what it means to be 'Korean' can be seen more distinctly if Japanese, Korean and Taiwanese (i.e. Chinese) management styles are compared by a simple model:

Concept		**Country**	
	Japan	*Korea*	*Taiwan*
Position and Authority	Low	High	Medium
Manager Co-ordination	High	Medium	Low
Loyalty to Organisation	High	High	Medium/Low

This demonstrates significant differences between the three races which become clearer when the concepts are explained in more detail:

1. **Position and Authority**
   In large Korean companies, the personal authority based on a manager's rank or position is very high. Management is authoritarian with a vertical hierarchy. This is very different to Japan, where despite the importance of seniority, management style is much less authoritarian and various levels of man-

agers are involved during their consensual decision-making activities. In Taiwan the 'Chinese' approach lies midway between the Korean and Japanese extremes.

2. **Manager Co-ordination**
   Manager co-ordination is defined as the amount of discussion required before the person in authority actually makes the decision. Japan is an extreme case as there is extremely high co-ordination amongst the staff and managers involved. Plans are made in detail and every possible eventuality is considered. Koreans take decisions more quickly and hence are regarded as medium in terms of manager co-ordination. The Taiwanese style is much more flexible, and has low manager co-ordination, which is indicative of the Chinese race's entrepreneurial nature. It is also attributed to the fact that the Taiwanese have smaller corporations than the Japanese and Koreans. Their limited size provides the chance for greater flexibility and rapid entry into new product areas. This strategy has been helpful in their penetration of world markets.

3. **Loyalty to Organisation**
   Both Japan and Korea tend to have high loyalty to the organisation. This is not just to the company, but also to other institutions such as their high school, university and even government. People not only identify with their organisation but show significant pride and loyalty. It can be seen in practice, by allegiance to a company motto, singing the corporate song, representation at company sporting events and sacrifice of leisure time to support the organisation in time of need. The Taiwanese and Chinese communities throughout the world have a reputation of being 'quick on their feet' to exploit a business opportunity, and this fits well with their approach of

loyalty to an idea or concept, rather than to the rigid structural traditions of the organisation.

ANALOGIES BETWEEN EUROPE AND ASIA

Another way for European managers to distinguish between the management styles of the three major Asian economies in Japan, Korea and Taiwan, is to compare them to the styles found in some of the various European countries. Just as Asian managers are acutely aware of differences in Asian cultures, values, management and leadership, so European managers are conscious of the differences that exist between the nations of Western Europe. A broad picture of the analogy between Europe and Asia is shown below:

Asia	**Europe**
Japan	Great Britain
	Germany
Korea	Italy
	Ireland
Taiwan	Holland
	Switzerland

This might seem strange at first glance, but there is some logic behind the comparisons which may help the European manager understand the behaviour of his welcoming business partners when he visits those Far Eastern countries for the first time:

1. **Japan**
   As an island nation, the Japanese have many similarities to the British and their geographical separation from the mainland hinders their social interaction with neighbouring countries. Both the

British and the Japanese have a patient, relatively subdued and cautious approach to management and decision-making.

The Japanese, however, also have characteristics similar to the German people. The Germans have the reputation throughout Europe and the rest of the world for their ability to move fast and effectively with excellent organisation once decisions are taken. They are also both skilled at taking concepts and projects through to a successful conclusion.

2. **Korea**

The Korean way of life and culture has a 'Latin' flavour and demonstrates similarities to Italy. Both Korea and Italy are peninsulas and share a common enjoyment of garlic in their cuisine. In terms of management style and behaviour of society, they have an unorganised and sometimes apparently chaotic approach to the task in hand! Italians and Koreans also share a passionate nature, and are prone to extreme emotions which can cloud judgement of major decisions. This results, as many will know, in business conclusions which sometimes defy normal logic.

Koreans have often been called the 'Irish of Asia' which refers to their gregarious nature and enjoyment of alcoholic beverages, rather than common burdens in their histories. *So-ju* is to Koreans as Guinness is to the Irish!

3. **Taiwan**

The Chinese, in general, and Taiwanese, in particular, have built up a reputation in Asia as being amongst the most effective business people. As a result, Taiwan could be compared to Holland or Switzerland. They are all small countries with limited population, but have become wealthy by steady business and economic success. Taiwan now has the highest foreign reserves per head of population in the world and is second only to Japan in terms of total foreign reserves held. This is a fine indication of their dedication to economic growth and prudent financial housekeeping.

KOREA, CHINA AND ASEAN

In the 1990s and beyond, Korean export markets will shift increasingly away from dependency upon the USA (a situation which has been predominant since the end of World War Two) towards playing a major role within Asia itself. Korean businesses and the Korean economy are now sufficiently large and technically advanced enough to be a provider of expertise and technology to the rest of the Asian continent. In turn, China and ASEAN (the Association of Southeast Asian Nations, comprising Thailand, Malaysia, Indonesia, Brunei, Singapore and the Philippines) will tend to provide bases for low-cost labour and manufacturing for Korean companies.

1. **China**
   This enormous country, with its 1.2 billion inhabitants, is a mystery not only for the rest of Asia, but also for the entire world. It is too early to forecast with any confidence whether China will reawaken and once again become the economic, business and political force it was many years ago. It does, however, provide an abundant low-cost labour market and also consumes a variety of low-price goods. The one major factor that is now different in the case of China's future business growth, is that of the significant role being played by other Asian countries and businesses.
   Whereas in the past, the USA was the major provider of loans, grants and aid to the development of

Japan and then Korea, today it is these two Asian countries who are taking a lead in providing business capital, technology transfer and other skills to China. The whole Asian and Pacific Rim region is expanding its economic alliance and beginning to operate as one trading bloc. This is in contrast to the old traditional dependency on the USA.

2. **ASEAN**
The ASEAN group of countries (except Singapore which is already one of South East Asia's success stories) are next in line to become the latest 'dragons' or newly industrialised countries of Asia. Although probably not all at the same pace, they will begin to follow Japan, Korea and Taiwan into faster economic development and provide excellent business opportunities for the rest of the world. Development in the ASEAN region is analogous to Japan in the late 1960s and early 70s, and Korea in the late 1970s and early 80s. Like their Japanese counterparts, Korean businesses have begun to increase their investment into these ASEAN countries. The major civil engineering project which constructed the long bridge between the Malaysian mainland and island of Penang is a well known early example.

KOREA'S *CHAEBOL*

In a similar way to Japan's 'zaibatsu' (*Keiretsu*), or large business empires, Korea's own huge business enterprises, the *Chaebol*, have been the key to the developing industrial environment in Korea. The *Chaebol* are highly diversified conglomerates which grew rapidly as a result of Korea's economic policies. These were aimed at boosting export markets to fuel the country's growth (see Chapter 3). There are a number of fundamental differences in the way that these *Chaebol* are managed, often indicative of the varying management styles of their founders. Some examples can be shown by summarising a few aspects of the four largest *Chaebol*, all of which have names which are familiar to households around the world.

Samsung

Although presently enjoying sales of over $50 billion dollars per annum, Samsung's Chairman Lee plans to increase these markedly, to $200 billion dollars by the year 2000 making his company one of the ten largest companies in the world. Unusually for Korea, he is making optimum use of highly trained professional managers, based on merit and performance, rather than relying upon family relatives and traditional connections. The major strategy of the Samsung corporation is to become more internationally orientated and to decentralise decision-making processes. The aim is to become the market leader in every field of business it enters.

Hyundai

The Hyundai corporation provides the best example of the authoritarian and chaotic management style present in many Korean companies. Its decision-making processes are hierarchical in nature, and Hyundai is largely run by the founder, Chung Ju-Yung, his brother, Chung Sae-Yung, together with his sons, the 'Chung family'. The former Chairman, Chung Ju-Yung, also ran for President in the 1992 election, almost in the style of America's Ross Perot! Although unsuccessful in his bid, he did enough to shake up the traditional political scene. Chung's management style is aggressive, and has been likened to a bulldozer by some industrial commentators. Of all the *Chaebol* chiefs, he is the one who probably wields most influence in the execution of business strategy.

Goldstar

Goldstar is a good example of a steady, calm and conservatively run company. Like Hyundai, major decision-making is undertaken by the founder's family and close associates. However, the management style is much more prudent by Korean standards, and the corporate philosophy can probably best be described as 'harmony'.

Daewoo

As mentioned earlier, Daewoo's Chairman Kim Woo-Choong is one of Korea's most respected businessmen. Unlike the other three major *Chaebol*, Daewoo was founded as recently as 1967, and in just twenty-six years has become an international player with sales in excess of $20 billion dollars per annum. There is a mystique surrounding the Chairman, and his superhuman qualities. Daewoo is famous for risk taking, and steps boldly where even other Korean corporations fear to tread. This includes countries such as Libya and Sudan. Management style is energetic and driven by the charismatic Kim. The company philosophy centres on working for pride not pleasure.

The *Chaebol*'s Future

One weakness perceived to be held by all Korea's conglomerates, is that they are far too diversified and dabble in every conceivable business sector, from aerospace to cars, to construction, to textiles and to foods. During the 1990s they will need to specialise on the core businesses and focus their individual strengths, if they are to continue their phenomenal success in world markets. This specialisation has already begun, with corporations such as Samsung concentrating on such growth industries as electronics and aerospace. During the next decade, the trend is expected to continue as the Korean government shifts from its former role as subsidiser and overseer of the *Chaebol*, to a new position, as regulator of their activities.

Despite the various differences between the leading *Chaebol*, there are numerous aspects which make them very 'Korean' in terms of their business style. These characteristics are ambition, willingness to sacrifice everything for the company and a desire to finish a project on time, all of which are driven by an emotion and passion seldom seen in Asia. They combine to make up a Korean management style which is an attractive option for foreign companies who are looking for business partners on the Pacific Rim.

6
Business Etiquette

Spilled rice grains can still be picked up again, but words once spoken are difficult to take back.

Korean proverb

TRULY KOREAN

Korean business practice has evolved as another branch of the country's cultural development, and that branch is very firmly part of the tree which has grown from traditional Confucian principles. Any relationship with a Korean business partner should be built using these principles and be seen by both sides as a long-term commitment. Although there are similarities between the social ethics of Japan and Korea, the traditional cultural background plays a greater part in Korean business etiquette than it does in Japan. It should be appreciated that Koreans do not like to be thought of as a latter-day Japan. Korean pride points out, sometimes quite forcefully, that much of Japan's culture reached their islands by crossing the Eastern Sea from the Korean peninsula.

However, because of Korea's isolation from the rest of the world for so many years, it does lie behind Japan in its understanding of global business. Although this lack of international experience has been a disadvantage, Koreans do demonstrate three important cultural advantages over their neighbours. First, their outgoing nature means they are likely to feel more at ease in the presence of foreigners than the Japanese. Second, their extraordinary 'we can do' work ethic, which has derived from their desire to overtake North Korean development and to catch up with Japan as fast as possible. Third, the overwhelming urge to better themselves economically and materially with their enthusiasm to adopt and adapt imported technology. As a result, Koreans and Westerners have the opportunity to feel comfortable and relaxed in each other's company. This is the critical precursor to the development of harmonious business and personal relationships.

The Korean nation's inbuilt desire to continue the evolution of their own special civilization means that, both consciously and subconsciously, Confucian principles become transferred to Government and industrial business policies. This is one reason why business in Korea must be regarded differently to that in Japan. The phrase 'Where Confucius wears a three-piece suit' should be regarded as a serious statement of business reality and not just a humorous comment upon the relationship between everyday office uniform and Korea's social past.

Before examining the key parts of business etiquette, it is worth emphasising that the Korean family system extends into many Korean firms. Indeed, it can be said that the 'Clan' has such an important role that the companies are staffed and managed as a type of family unit. Because Confucian principles demand harmonious personal relationships, the presence of blood relatives within the structure raises the chances of successful co-operation and consensus agreement in decision-making processes. It potentially reduces competition and chances of conflict between managers. Even the most dynamic of Korean enterprises fosters a paternal spirit towards their employees, with bonuses paid deliberately at times of high expense, such as Summer Holiday, *Chusok* (Autumn Harvest Festival) and at New Year. This same family concern will also be shown for staff's special personal needs, such as a funeral or children's school expenses. It is a traditional Korean solution to circumstances created by the Korean cultural environment.

ELEMENTS OF ETIQUETTE

Formal business etiquette can be broken down into a set of important elements, which should be committed to memory by all those who interact with Koreans in business or government. They should be regarded as a set of rules which will help smooth the path of negotiation, communication and partnership.

A **Formal Introduction** is the precursor to a successful first meeting. It is courteous to arrange the meeting well in advance and inform the people of the subjects on your agenda. It may be helpful to include positioning papers in English and Korean, particularly if the matters to be discussed have a legal, financial or technical content. The potential business partner also likes to prepare in advance and doesn't want to appear unco-operative after hearing a detailed presentation, in what is likely to be his second or maybe third language. Additional help for this first formal introduction can be realised by using an intermediary or local Korean consultant. This is an effective way for two potential partners to learn something about each other prior to the first meeting. As personal connections are so important in Korean business, the intermediary can lay the foundation for the beginning of the relationship. Employment of such a consultant can be expensive upfront but, in the long term, a very cost-effective way of progressing a new venture. A consultant, trusted and respected by both sides, will undoubtedly be further used to help negotiation or partner disagreements as the business relationship grows.

First meetings with Koreans are important. Initial impressions score heavily and the whole session needs to be handled with patience, sensitivity, good humour and a positive attitude to generate good *Kibun*.

The **Business Card** is an essential part of Korean life! A card can be printed quickly and inexpensively through a hotel on arrival, but to avoid wasting valuable time, it is better obtained in advance of the visit. Your company, name, title, position and professional qualifications should be printed on one side of the card, with the equivalent information given in *Hangul* on the other. Pay careful attention to the description of your position. The potential Korean business partner will wish to know your status and want to place this within your own company's organisation. The description will need to be meaningfully translated into a Korean equivalent. Avoid use of job names such as Scientific Officer or Senior Administrative Assistant. They will mean little to those who work in a rigid hierarchical arrangement such as is found throughout Korean enterprises.

Business cards are exchanged at the beginning of the meeting after a handshake. Cards are given and received with the right hand, or both hands, and it is polite to accompany the exchange with a slight bow. If the meeting involves a number of people, it is useful to arrange the cards in front of you in the same format as the participants around the table. It's not unknown for a visitor to sit down with six Mr. Kims or Mr. Lees, so to have their titles and family names to hand can be invaluable! During the meeting, the newly acquired business cards must not be used as notepads. Defacing the cards in this way is considered to be rude.

Building Relationships comes naturally to a Korean business man as it is the pivot around which all Korean enterprises operate. For a Korean, the most important aspect of a business partnership is the relationship itself. This conflicts with the Western viewpoint which emphasises the business and profit motive as being of much greater consequence. A relationship in Korea depends not just on friendship between partners but also the commonality of background. If a common school, university or acquaintances are shared, then the relationship stands a greater chance of strengthening through trust and sharing of the same experiences.

The foreigner who wants to succeed with a business venture in Korea must somehow adapt to the system of relationships. Whilst he cannot share the same university, he can develop sensitivity and understanding which will help build a sound alliance. This requires time, patience and diplomacy. Decisions must not be rushed and the slower the overall process the more likely the outcome will be beneficial to both partners. Perhaps better to target to earn a 'slow Won' rather than a 'fast Buck'! It is worth adding here that although a written contract between partners is a binding agreement to a Westerner, in the Korean mind it is just a reflection of the feelings that exist at the time, between the individuals who actually signed their names – a statement of the relationship. If that relationship is not continually being fostered, strengthened and replenished, then the contract can become a worthless piece of paper. It is, therefore, important that foreigners who do business in Korea are prepared to commit considerable personal effort from the outset into creating the business association. The importance of staff continuity and consistent visible goals from the foreign enterprise cannot be overstressed. This is a concept that a Head Office in London, Paris or New York sometimes has difficulty in grasping.

Entertainment plays an integral role in any business engagement, and is almost always an all-male activity. This can be a constant source of annoyance to the expatriate wife who sits at home wondering what devious things Korean business partners are plotting for her husband in the restaurants and night clubs of Seoul or Pusan! Business dinners are frequent, usually too frequent for the visitor, and normally follow on directly after a late finish at the office. They are occasions when Koreans dispense with the formality of the office environment and take on the seriously enjoyable activities of eating, drinking and interacting to build the personal relationships. The foreigner's alcohol consumption capacity may be a deciding factor to a successful ongoing business negotiation, but this may not be as daunting as one imagines, as Koreans have a low alcohol threshold capacity and usually drink too fast! Neat Scotch whisky is the most popular drink, but budgetary constraints may limit expenditure to locally distilled whisky or the pleasant dinner wine *Pop-ju* or the local 'fire-water' *So-ju*. Whatever happens, it is most important to relax and enjoy the occasion. Natural reserve should be cast aside in favour of having a good time.

Hostesses, often one to each guest, are provided at some establishments. They are trained to pamper to the customer's every whim and will be humorously sympathetic to a foreigner's stumbling attempts with chopsticks or his eyeballs spinning whilst eating the hottest *Kimchi*. At the most expensive and lavish of dinners, these *Kisaeng* girl hostesses will wear *Hanbok* national dress. Apart from their good looks, the girls are also picked for their vibrant personality and ability to sing and dance.

Singing is an important part of many dinners and the visitor is expected to participate fully. It is another part of the unwinding process. A good baritone or tenor voice, whilst an advantage, is not an essential prerequisite. The message is simple – burst forth with unbridled enthusiasm and belt out any popular song, even if you are tone deaf! A lousy voice is not a serious handicap, even if the Koreans in your party all seem to be budding Pavarottis. They are a musical race and have been brought up from children on a diet of singing, as well as rice and *Kimchi*. A foreigner who really wants to make an impression on his partners will learn a Korean song. *Arirang* would be a good choice as it is loved by all Koreans and has an easily memorised melody.

An evening's entertainment may well extend beyond the dinner into a night club or bar, which gives further opportunity to let the hair down and learn more about the Korean business partner and city night-life. The following day, the possible crazy excesses of the previous night are forgotten and usually not even discussed. Best not to mention a hangover either, as admittance that *So-ju* has given you a rotten headache would be to lose face! A successful evening will unquestionably lead to closer relationships and it can do wonders for *Kibun*!

If you are hosting a dinner party yourself, it is probably best to avoid the main hotels. Take the advice of Korean colleagues as to the best restaurants. There are thousands in Seoul and Korea's other major cities and your partners will have their favourites, where they know they can obtain high quality at reasonable cost.

Before leaving the subject of entertainment it is worth emphasising that Koreans will go to great lengths to ensure hospitality for their visitors. This can sometimes be overwhelming and can leave the unwary embarrassed. A gesture towards balancing this generosity can be achieved by bringing gifts. Imagination and a little detective work can help identify the most suitable gift, but if all else fails, an excellent fall back is good quality Scotch whisky.

The **Personal Touch** is the element which can elevate a good relationship into one which has all the credentials for moving forward into a meaningful and long-term business venture. Skill, patience, humour and sensitivity are required to develop a successful personal touch, but it will be worth every minute of the effort. It will boost the morale of partners and employees and be seen as sympathetic to the largely paternalistic style of Korean organisations.

The first step is to learn as much as possible about the personal interests and families of the Korean staff, without appearing to be nosey! Encourage reciprocation by telling people about your own family and hobbies. A few family photographs, particularly of children, help this enormously. Express an interest in Korean way of life, culture, sport, art, music, theatre and countryside. This is no hardship as much of it is extremely absorbing. Koreans are immensely proud of their heritage and will be delighted at the interest. Expect to be invited out to their favourite haunts for further exploration.

Praise and more praise during daily interaction leads to

constant warm feelings and fosters good *Kibun*. This doesn't mean to say that criticism is never acceptable, but it must be used with great care otherwise face-loss can damage relationships. Before any meeting starts, an adroit visitor will set the scene with good news and congratulatory messages.

Patience and Tolerance are the hardest skills to develop. Head office can be breathing fire and brimstone down your neck for a quick result whilst the Korean business partner is prevaricating over apparently minor clauses in a deal. This is a time for adopting the gentle, firm but authoritative approach of the traditional Korean *Yangban* classes. Pushing too hard can lead to breakdown and it is an opportunity for the delicate personal touch to steer a careful course through the difficulties in order to reach a solution.

Harmony within all human relationships, absolute respect for authority and an inbuilt feeling for Korean nationalism are the foundation of traditional Confucianism. The desire for harmony features strongly in Korean business ethics and is based partly upon a corporate paternalistic attitude to staff by senior managers in the organisation and partly by the significant loyalty of the employees.

The never-ending quest for harmony means that the relationships between all levels of staff, vertically and horizontally, in the Korean company are vitally important. The foreigner working with or within that company must seek equally hard to achieve the same level of trust and respect with his or her Korean colleagues. What makes the Korean situation different from the Japanese, is that loyalty to the person or manager is of much greater significance than loyalty to the company. Harmony within the personal relationship, based upon honour and integrity, encourages staff to follow their manager and mentor from one company to another. The foreigner needs to remember this point, and use it to advantage when recruiting Korean nationals for a branch office, agency or joint venture.

The urge to achieve and then maintain harmony is so strong that on occasions it will take priority over sensible business considerations – another time when Western logic fails!

The naive visitor can easily fall into the trap of believing that Korean partners are being bloody-minded over a simple business decision or transaction. In reality, they may be doing nothing more than fiercely protecting group harmony within their organisation.

COMMUNICATION

Communicating across deeply differing cultures as well as between languages adds a new dimension to business arrangements and particularly negotiation. The comprehension level of English-speaking Koreans will almost certainly be lower than suggested by their behaviour. The foreigner compounds the situation by speaking too quickly and using too many colloquial expressions. What can confuse Koreans even further is the variety of English dialects. A broad city or rural dialect can unwittingly lead to a total communication breakdown. Because of the natural politeness of the Koreans, they will be unlikely to ask for a statement to be repeated or qualified. The result can be a complete misinterpretation which can be a severe setback in striking up a business alliance.

The foreigner should use all his powers and senses to cross the communication barrier. Key points should always be emphasised and repeated, slowly if necessary. Eyes and ears should be used skilfully to judge the success or failure of the spoken word! If an interpreter is being used, try and ensure he (or she) is briefed beforehand on the background, structure and nature of the proposals. It is equally important to allow the interpreter copious time during a meeting to explain and clarify the substance of the proposal, and your response to any counter-proposal from the Korean side. Never hurry, as it will be seen as a sign of impatience, and maybe even a hint that the truth is being masked.

Anyone who has spent time working with Koreans will know that they much prefer to communicate in their own language, particularly between themselves. It is quite common for all English language communication to stop for ten or fifteen minutes whilst the Korean team, including the interpreter, attempt to clarify the situation, discuss possible responses and then decide in which way the response will be given. This is a cue for supreme patience by the foreigner and not a time to look repeatedly at a watch or irritably drum fingers on the table! An understanding of even a little of the Korean language can be very valuable at moments like this. As well as giving a rudimentary feel of the nature of their discussion, it is a tactical advantage in a serious negotiation if the Koreans know you can grasp something of what is being said. To reduce the chances of misunderstanding and resultant confusion, it is helpful to write and, if possible, exchange notes after important meetings. If negotiations are critical to success on both sides, this can be taken a stage further by providing detailed minutes written in English and Korean.

Patience and sympathy for the Korean viewpoint are great virtues for foreigners who are in communication with Korean companies. In times of difficulty and disagreement, it is essential that lines of communication remain open. This can be achieved through the more junior ranks, even if there are dreadful problems at the highest levels in the organisation. Communication breakdown must never be allowed to occur, a point which may need on occasions to be stressed quite forcibly back to the foreigner's Head office.

One communication problem that is sure to cause confusion for the foreigner is the fact that Koreans will naturally give a negative response to a negative question. For example, if the question is 'Don't you know the Five Year

Plan?' The response could be 'Yes – you are correct, I don't know the Plan', rather than the expected reply of 'No, I don't know the Plan'. All visitors to Korea must prepare themselves for this, it happens frequently and will cause embarrassment to both sides. However, at least partial avoidance can be achieved by phrasing questions in a positive format, such as 'Do you know the Five Year Plan?'

NEGOTIATION

'It takes two to tango' so the saying goes, and in Korea the dance can be difficult to learn and even more difficult to perform successfully – even though the two partners have a common interest in performing the steps in harmony! Koreans are tough negotiators and will work tirelessly to achieve the best possible deal for themselves. They hold the view that the foreign business man and investor has plenty to give and can be progressively worn down to yield more, as surely as water eventually erodes the hardest of rocks. Negotiation in Korea is yet another part of the relationship-building exercise and will reveal, hopefully, the foreigner's commitment to the task in hand and the long-term future of the business deal or enterprise.

A wise foreign company will field a strong and senior team for critical negotiation issues. This demonstrates the important nature of the possible deal. As negotiation is always a time-consuming exercise, the same wise company will have quietly allowed hours, maybe days, within their schedule to progress and complete the deal. Koreans are superbly skilled at brinkmanship and may delay yielding anything critical until the last possible moment. This is due to their confident expectation that the rushed foreign executive will always give way on a key issue just prior to his headlong drive to reach the airport in time for his return flight to Europe. They are often right!

Good negotiators must also be creative in their approach. The 'Patience of Job' is not always good enough and will not necessarily yield results. Innovative planning can plot a path to the desired objective and different ways it might be achieved by incentives and trade-offs. Always have alternatives prepared and ready for use. The Koreans will have their own objectives planned and these will include those 'infernal ones that defy Western logic'. In any negotiated venture they will seek to achieve considerable influence in ongoing operations, avoid face loss in any shape or form on the way, look for maximum and ongoing technology transfer, growing personal relationships and a situation which potentially leads to long-term growth and export potential. Judicious use of a local consultant prior to negotiation can help this exercise considerably. He can research the local market situation, attitude and feelings of the potential partners and any government departments which may be involved in approving the deal. This same consultant may also be used as a facilitator or interpreter in key contractual meetings. In the event of negotiation breakdown, which is not uncommon, he can be used as the vital communication link to regenerate and rebuild a suitable negotiating relationship.

Entertainment may play an important part in the negotiation exercise – before, during and after the deal is struck and contract signed. It will help the 'feel good' *Kibun* factor and genuinely reveal more about both the Korean partners and yourself. The personal contact and shared experience of a good meal and excellent night out will make continued negotiation and meeting of the minds that much easier. Negotiation is rarely completed in one session or visit by the foreign company, so it is sound practice to always end on a high note with past achievements emphasised and the promise of bigger and better things to come.

UNDERSTAND THE KOREAN VIEWPOINT

A concerted effort to understand the Korean viewpoint will unquestionably assist in building bridges across the cultural gap between Occidental and Oriental. Communication and negotiation will become easier and lead to closer personal relationships and then a more harmonious partnership. Although Koreans strive for internationalisation and the economic advantage it brings, they also strongly defend their independence and unique identity. This means they have an inherent fear of domination by foreign businesses and multinational corporations. Koreans have been successful in achieving this goal throughout centuries of adversity and are, therefore, overtly sensitive about possible loss of control in a partnership with a foreign company. This fear must not be underestimated, particularly if the Korean company is one which is still autocratically managed by its founder. He will have 'sweated blood' to make his enterprise succeed in the face of fierce local opposition and will fight tooth and nail to prevent loss of control to a foreign partner through a poorly negotiated joint venture. Emotion could well take precedent over sound business common sense!

This same Korean company may also operate as a sort of family association. Key positions within its organisation may be held by immediate family members or close relatives. Potential foreign partners should undertake research into the organisation of the enterprise to establish what family or 'clan' structure exists. As mentioned earlier, such a family unit provides ongoing management stability. Persuading the family to give up some control is a threat to that stability and must be accounted for within any business negotiation which takes place.

So conflicting objectives are almost certain to arise between the partners at early stages in negotiation or partnership. There is no simple solution, but if the foreigner can understand that the Koreans may wish to prioritise the importance of steady growth on a broad base, maximising export growth with minimum impact on imports and maintaining as much management control as possible, then he will have a good chance of manoeuvring negotiations to strike the right deal.

Once the contract is signed, the relationship and its fruitful development begin in earnest. The foreign company must see it only as a necessary preamble before reaching the official start-line. From the Korean viewpoint, it is a very personal agreement that can change with new circumstances and new people. So perhaps the ultimate challenge for those who draw up the contract is to create words in both languages which are clear and unambiguous, but also adaptable to changes which might arise on both sides of the partnership. A challenge indeed!

One subjective way to help understand the Korean viewpoint is to become tuned to what is happening in everyday Korean society, both on the streets and inside the partner's company. As a major developing country, Korea is undergoing a period of enormous change. Its unprecedented economic growth is putting tremendous stress on the people as they begin to come to terms with changes in technology, diet, role of women, fashion, transport, housing and a significant increase in disposable income. Much of this is alien to the culture and beliefs of their forefathers. By watching, listening and talking to Koreans in all sections of their society, the visitor can learn a lot about the life-force of modern Korea and how its industry and people are coping with internationalisation and the trappings of materialism. It will all help, and the new found knowledge is likely to be appreciated by Koreans in the partnership.

7
Working with Koreans

One moment of patience may ward off disaster
One moment of impatience may ruin a whole life

Korean proverb

CROSSING CULTURAL BOUNDARIES

Cross-cultural training in business management, industrial relations and communication etiquette can partially prepare the foreign manager for working with Koreans in a branch office, agency relationship or joint venture. But what this training often fails to deliver is the need to become sensitive to the real human situation which may exist within the company. It can also fail to prepare the foreigner for the emotional stress of living and working with a company whose way of life, motives, decision-making processes, staff turnover and dynamic rate of change are so very different.

Coming to terms with these alien and sometimes very disturbing circumstances will be a major task, and some fall by the wayside after acrimonious arguments which can lead to complete corporate communication failure. Disputes with employees can occasionally become very serious. During one rancorous pay disagreement in the Seoul branch of a multinational bank, the foreign manager was barricaded in his office. The story goes that the Korean unionised staff banged cymbals and drums outside his office until the police arrived half an hour later!

STATUS INSIDE THE COMPANY

Traditionally, management in a Korean company is autocratic and the extent to which this operates may come as a surprise to a new foreigner. Status is extremely important and there is a strict hierarchy stretching down from the president through the multiple levels of managers to the office or shop floor. Promotion depends upon age as well as ability and this is evident to a much greater degree than in a Western company. Status can be very visible and will be seen by position of offices within the building, their size, and quality of furniture and carpets. The most loyal 'company man' will manoeuvre his desk close to the seats of power! If in any doubt as to the seniority of Koreans within an organisation, it is worth observing who sits in the right hand rear seat of a car. That position is reserved for the person of highest status within the group travelling in the car. The person of lowest status is likely to be in the front passenger seat.

To make life more difficult for the newcomer, social status may also be in operation. There are traditional upper, middle and lower classes in Korea, stemming from ancestry, place of birth, schooling and universities attended. There are rules of etiquette between these classes and senior staff within a company may not wish to be seen putting their social status into question, by dealing with, or promoting, someone of the wrong background or class. This situation is less prevalent than in the past, but may be evident in the more traditional Korean companies.

So where does the foreigner fit into this structure? It is important that his rank is clearly identified on arrival, and the higher the rank the better. Dependent upon age, experience, rank and title, he will be slotted into a particular level in the minds of the Korean executives. His actual behaviour within his role, inside the office and in dealing with others in business and social activities, will allow the Koreans to place his 'class' in society. In ordinary circumstances, this is likely to lie between the middle and upper strata.

In a typical Korean office, therefore, staff members can be bound in a mind-blowing tangle of social class, company status, personal ties and relationships. Groups and friendships are likely to be formed on the basis of regional background, school classmates, military friendships and particularly university affiliations. For example, a Korean company president who studied at Seoul National University – the highest ranking university in Korea – may strongly favour recruiting new graduate staff from this same institution. There may still be strong personal relationships between a graduate and his university professor.

The naive expatriate can, of course, arrive and completely upset the apple-cart by recruiting someone of an unsuitable social background, whose ability may have been largely judged by the quality of his spoken and written English. This same expatriate can further compound his problems by firing an employee who is the lynchpin around which a key internal group structure revolves. A final blow may follow if the new foreigner reorganises the company structure by reducing layers of management in a typical European manner. The antagonism which is likely to come from this meddling and interference will affect company operations significantly and potentially lead to severance of personal relationships and crumbling communication.

Apart from ensuring he researches and becomes aware of the internal structure of the Korean enterprise, the foreigner can maximise his chances of success by using the knowledge and often significant skill of his secretary. Quality Korean secretaries are usually graduates and are worth their weight in gold in building bridges across the mysteries of cross-cultural divide. They can be astute, wise ladies and often have a much better grasp of Western ways than Korean men. The secretary can act as communicator, translator, cultural adviser and 'confidante' in addition to her undertaking normal office duties. If close and trusted relationships are built between the two, the effectiveness and status of the foreigner within the organisation will grow visibly. She is also likely to keep him up-to-date with company bar-room and lunch table gossip!

WORKING HOURS

Korea has always had the reputation of operating one of the longest working weeks in the world. Although the formal number of hours worked slowly declines, in practice for many staff, including expatriates, it will be well in excess of fifty hours per week. Many companies still work at least two part or whole Saturdays each month. Sometimes a free weekend will be taken for staff orientation and training, and possibly be residential in a country or mountainous area.

Many employees start their working day early, a practice particularly noticeable if the senior Korean executives also happen to begin at the crack of dawn. Lunch time is usually quite rigid. At the appropriate hour, the office staff seem to evaporate in an instant, and gravitate towards staff canteen or the local restaurants. Koreans need timely refuelling and that means more *Kimchi* and rice! In the evening, the office seems to just work on and on. This is particularly noticeable if there are sales teams in operation. The salesmen will be returning back to the office from late afternoon onwards to record their day's efforts. Many of the most loyal staff will insist on staying until the most senior employees have departed rather than lose face by being seen to leave 'early'. The expatriate secretary will almost certainly fall into this loyal category and she will stay until the daily chores are finished.

PRODUCTIVITY

Although working hours and the meetings within them can be interminably long, and annual holiday allowances seem woefully inadequate, overall productivity within the company can be very low. Time management doesn't appear to be a priority in a company which just extends its working day to achieve the tasks in hand. The 'tiredness factor' is clearly visible around the office but is completely ignored as staff toil inefficiently onwards. However, as Korea internationalises and labour costs rise with the country's development, there is evidence that Korean companies will embrace Western techniques to raise productivity both within the office environment and on the shop floor. But even within a company which professes to have introduced more efficient working practices, there is always a danger that a short-term cost-cutting exercise on use of a photocopier or fax will jeopardise longer term strategic gains. The foreign manager must become tuned to this situation and encourage the best of productivity enhancement methods to fit with Korean management style. 'Koreanisation' of these western ways to achieve productivity gains is a hard-won skill – perhaps even Nirvana – but well worth the considerable labour and effort it will demand.

CONFIDENTIALITY

Well-kept secrets are a rare commodity inside the average Korean company. Salary levels appear to be known by everybody and the foreign manager may find keys for the office safe held by all and sundry! Koreans regard information relevant to the company as information which is equally important to their own well-being. So-called 'confidential' matters, therefore, tend to escape rapidly and with amazing accuracy. Should the foreigner wish to communicate highly confidential matters with his head office, then he is advised to do so through equipment in his own home or by previously arranged cryptic messages. Overnight incoming fax messages may be scrutinised at the office machine by inquisitive but well-meaning early starters prior to the foreign manager's arrival.

On a daily basis, some deft diplomacy may be required to keep personal matters private and confidential. The possibility of inflicting face-loss is always present if the foreigner deliberately attempts to withhold financial or technical information from certain of his Korean colleagues. Keeping information confidential from external sources is less difficult, although previous employees may well have been tempted to take sensitive technical data to their new and possibly rival companies. It should also be remembered that copyright and patent protection in Korea is still weaker in practice than all multinational companies would wish. The very act of registration of processes with the Government during technology transfer to Korea provides valuable data to would-be product copiers. Those transferring original technology would do well to err on the side of caution at all times.

MAKING DECISIONS

Decision-making processes in Korean companies generally involve considerable consultation within the strata of both middle and top management, although any decision of consequence will always be taken by the head of the company. To the foreigner working amidst these sometimes painfully slow exercises, the gift of patience must be regarded as heaven-sent. Only in small very autocratic companies can one expect rapid results, and in these cases it is usually the founder head who responds. He will have always made the decisions and will wish to continue to do so until he passes on the power to a younger member of his family. The expatriate executive should court comfortable and meaningful relationships at all levels in the company as each can provide significant input to the decision-making processes at varying levels of detail from everyday operation to longer term strategic planning. All these people have their part to play and in true Confucian fashion will prevaricate if their own position is threatened by potential loss of 'face'. Group harmony must be preserved and decision-making will be delayed to maintain that status quo, no matter how painstakingly the common sense of western logic is expressed.

The situation in Government decision-making is even more extreme but follows the same lines. Often the process will begin at the lowest possible departmental levels and trickle slowly upwards with seemingly infinite detail being examined microscopically at every step. Nobody in these departments wants the blame for any mistake falling upon their shoulders. There are opportunities here for the skills of those in the junior ranks of the Korean company to leap these government hurdles and expedite the decision-making processes, through personal skills, entertainment and other traditional Korean methods. In all these relationships with the government, it is usually better to let the Korean employees dictate methods of approach, even if they seem long-winded. Many of them will be very experienced in achieving their objectives successfully.

GETTING PAID

Many Korean companies with decent paper profits have gone bankrupt due to high account receivables which just could not be collected. It has even been known for companies to inject more resources into collection of debts than into promotion of their products. At times, it seems that withholding of payments is a national sport where thrust and counter-thrust is used to pressurise the guilty parties. As often in Korea, there is no simple solution to the problem, but the foreigner must be aware that it will be happening and the staff in his own organisation may be masters at the game! He must always be cautious of any promise to pay to a schedule and insist on confirmed irrevocable letters of credit on every possible occasion.

KOREAN EDUCATION AND ITS RESULTS

Koreans have a passion for education and the country boasts one of the highest literacy rates in the world. However, measured by European standards, the methods of learning are largely by rote. This system drives the student towards cramming to achieve exam results good enough to enter one of Korea's most prestigious universities. Should they fail to gain sufficient marks for entry to Seoul National, the nation's number one, students hope they will be good enough for other major universities such as Yonsei, Korea or, for women students, Ehwa. The annual entrance examination event leads to considerable family stress, particularly if the student fails to meet expectations. Suicide by student or parent is not unknown.

These principles of education tend to produce graduates who lack a western style of an enquiring, creative mind and a personality which fails to challenge long-held outdated beliefs. This is very apparent in the Korean office environment. The situation is worsened even further in strictly traditional companies where good ideas originating in the junior ranks rarely make it to the top. Confucian principles of respect to those in authority mean that these young employees fear their elders would lose face for not initiating the idea themselves. Times are slowly changing, particularly in the more progressive *Chaebol*, but lack of creativity is still very noticeable.

STAFF RECRUITMENT

Because of the complex network of personal relationships in Korean society, head-hunting or scouting through friend or family contacts is the primary method of recruitment, particularly for professional, graduate or more senior executive positions. Executive search, as it is known in the West, is not extensively used. It is noticeable that even Korean company directors can become personally involved in the interviews and selection process of quite junior staff. This helps demonstrate a paternalistic approach and encourages the group harmony. A candidate's previous professor may well be contacted for proof of integrity, work rate and ability to fit with the company culture.

The foreigner working inside the company is advised to run with the system which is in operation. He can contribute in recruitment exercises by helping to define professional and technical role specification for the vacancy; including typical knowledge, skills and experience required. Placement of Western-style glossy adverts in the English language journals and newspapers could well be counter-productive, even offensive to Korean colleagues, and may not yield a significant response. However, the expatriate is likely to be welcomed by his partners to be part of the interview process and should use the opportunity to test candidates' innovative abilities and English communication skills, if they are relevant to the job. Koreans' written English is rarely as good as they speak and is worthy of concentrated examination during the selection process. This is particularly important if the role involves the presentation of written reports off-shore to the foreign partner's other international operations.

The more junior clerical jobs can be filled through classified advertising in appropriate newspapers. Careful job description is advisable as an initial screening exercise, otherwise the Company Personnel function may be overwhelmed with applications from unsuitable candidates.

Junior trainee secretarial staff may be employed by the same route, but it is likely that the executive expatriate will be looking for a far more qualified and experienced lady to act as his secretary, mentor and personal assistant. Recruitment of a high quality secretary may be one of the most important tasks undertaken during an assignment in Korea. The grapevine network of the Foreign Chambers of Commerce or maybe members of the Seoul Club provide possible routes of search, but it is usual to use the services of one of the secretarial employment agencies which exist in the major cities. They will supply c.v.s of candidates for interview. A secretary may, of course, come with the job if there is a succession change-over of an expatriate post. Whilst this may make a significant contribution to continuity, there is no absolute guarantee that the incoming manager will form a bond and successful working relationship with the incumbent lady. Loyalty to the person, in this case the previous manager, may take precedence over loyalty to the company and the secretary may soon search for new pastures.

STAFF DISMISSAL

Due to the paternalistic nature of much of Korean business and the sometimes overriding need to maintain group harmony, staff dismissal is a delicate and sensitive area. Preservation of face by the unfortunate dismissed employee is one of the goals. Very occasionally, face-loss in this situation can lead the dismissed person to take the ultimate sacrifice of suicide. There are rumours that such an attempt was made, using a knife, in a joint venture company a few years ago. Enormous discretion and patience along with a carefully laid plan is advisable and the skills of the local Korean executives can be used to execute severance in the most suitable way for all concerned. For employees of many years' service, generous separation or severance payments will be necessary and local advice should be sought. In general, these should considerably exceed the minimum levels of Korean Labour Laws, and it is an opportunity to demonstrate to all the caring and benevolent nature of company management.

Under-performers may be penalised by being repeatedly overlooked for promotion, even if they are in the right age group for a lift to the next level. Eventually, the message will penetrate and the employee will almost certainly resign his position. If he doesn't then transfer to another office or factory within the Korean partner's organisational structure can sometimes be used. This is also a way of giving a clear message to office trouble-makers who continue to challenge the establishment! The new position may just involve a long and tortuous commuter journey through Seoul's suburban traffic jams and persuade the employee to seek his fortune elsewhere.

FEMALE EMPLOYEES

Newcomers to Korea often comment that even the most progressive Korean companies seem to treat women with contempt. Gifts may be given to male employees at the achievement of a sales target, whilst the females receive nothing. Confucian tradition has always placed women in an inferior role and it was only in 1989 that the first Equal Employment Law was approved. In most instances, this has had little effect in the employment practices of male-dominated Korean firms. Many still pressurise women employees to resign immediately they marry, or at the very latest when they are pregnant. Very few will return after they have had their child. Women's salaries are also frequently less than men's for the equivalent job.

Korean women are fighting back but have a long journey to make. Some deliberately seek out employment with foreign joint ventures as these are seen to have a more liberal and forward-looking attitude to their plight. Such joint ventures need to beware of overreacting to this situation and employing too many women in anything other than clerical, administrative or factory shop-floor roles. Male chauvinism is only dying slowly and interfaces with traditional Korean enterprises and Government Ministries are best continued in the normal all-male environment. The female power base is still expected to be back at home with the family.

UNIONS

Korean workers are now the highest paid in Asia after Japan, and many have reason to be grateful to their unions for the successes achieved during the late 1980s in raising their salaries and standards of living. The Korean government has actively discouraged union activity, but perhaps due to some of the major confrontations in the *Chaebol* in recent years, has become more tolerant of these organised labour movements. Throughout industry, both management and workforce have realised the importance of retaining their international competitiveness, so negotiation and compromise have become the normal way to resolve differences. Under current law, only one union organisation is allowed to represent the workers in an industry or company, and unions are presently banned from participating in politics. By Western standards, their powers and overall organisation are weak and democratic reforms in the country's labour laws are high on their agenda for the 1990s. The unions are likely to pursue their objective through a lawful route, but in Korea this is by no means certain and violent measures can never be ruled out completely.

Foreign joint ventures will come across varying degrees of union activity dependent upon industry and size of Korean partner. Most company unions belong to a national or possibly local federation who represent their members using collective bargaining for employment welfare and wage hikes. Although the foreign influence in a joint venture may raise salaries above the local average, there should be no complacency that this will inevitably reduce the chances of union confrontation. Less tangible flashpoints can surface from time to time, perhaps due to interference in working methods by the foreign partner or maybe a perceived threat to national pride and dominance by a multinational corporation. Managers should be acutely aware of these subjective feelings of their employees and be ready to listen and negotiate to maintain harmony and comfortable manager–employee relationships. In this way, the Unions are less likely to cause embarrassing difficulties.

KOREAN EXECUTIVES

It's a warm sunny afternoon and after a heavy lunch, the senior Korean executive swivels his chair away from prying eyes outside his office. This is not to contemplate upon new sales and marketing initiatives or consider the five-year plan, but to have a quiet read of the daily paper followed by a sleep. Later on, he will consider visiting the barber shop in the basement of his high-rise office block, where he will have his hair clipped, fingernails manicured and a relaxing massage by his favourite young Miss Kim. This is just part of the lifestyle of senior Korean executives and absolutely infuriating to the newly arrived foreign manager who seems to be working twenty-four hours a day, seven days a week to launch the new business venture. Those cross-cultural relationships can easily become strained and it's always the Westerner who breaks first!

Harsh critics of Korean management style will say that there is little or no management at all, just self-preservation of the status and the power that goes with senior executive roles. In the more extreme cases, social class and status are taken to a further level where foreigners arriving in Korea are denied access to the very officials they have come to visit, all because they are perceived to be of too junior a rank. These are Confucian principles operating in their most extreme and traditional way. The importance of elevating job description status on one's business card can be clearly seen and use of words such as director or senior executive are recommended. This may be critical if a visit for negotiation or interview is being made to top management in one of Korea's *Chaebol*.

Changes to this rigid structure are in evidence within companies which are exposed to international competitive markets, and more flexible consensus management styles are being introduced in the best-run Korean firms. Although this may be a comforting thought for future generations of foreign businessmen in Korea, it may not help the frustrated present incumbent in a small joint venture partnership. In his situation, it is yet another case for demonstrating patient diplomacy, to be helped by slowly easing the Korean executives step-by-step into the management requirements of the foreign partner. As a result, they will progressively experience first-hand some of the advantages of Western-style techniques of, data collection and analysis, planning, inventory control, engineering maintenance, management by objectives, delegation and quality assurance. It is likely to be a slow and sometimes painful task, but the results may be surprisingly rewarding if handled with tact and empathy.

Before leaving the subject of Korean executives, their copious use of the 'chop' must be mentioned. The 'chop' is the personal seal or signature of the executive concerned and is used liberally to authorise documents and payment of bills. 'Chopping' is a time-consuming task, and in a shared joint venture, both Korean and foreign senior executives are likely to be kept busy with this approval process. Authorisation procedures must be carefully agreed between both partners, particularly in the light of Koreans' propensity for delaying payment for as long as possible. A foreigner must never assume that a bill will be rapidly paid as soon as his own 'chop' has put ink to paper. The bill might be held by the Korean team for weeks awaiting the final approval for payment. If this occurs frequently, loss of financial control of the Company's affairs may follow, leading to confusion and aggravation. Foreigner beware!

MOTIVATING STAFF

Confronted with alien aspects of management, organisation and behaviour, the newcomer to the venture or Korean company must study the overall situation and attempt to conform to what he sees and hears. Raising the morale of the local workforce should be one of his consuming priorities and a plan to achieve this should be based upon:

1. **Sound Remuneration**
   The company must have a salary structure. This is essential in a country where status and seniority are so critical. There should be policies and procedures, which are fully understood by all, so employees know where they are placed in the system, and what they might expect in the future. Policies for the bonus system, which typically pay extra 'months' of salary at certain times of year will be required, but should be performance related.

2. **Additional Benefits**
   If not already being practised, there ought to be some extra staff benefits created to demonstrate the paternalistic approach. These may be of the tangible sort in the form of scholarships, housing allowance, interest free loans for mortgage downpayments, car allowance, company bus transportation or subsidised

lunches. They can also be of a less tangible nature such as an invitation to a splendid New Year's Day luncheon, gifts for an employee's wedding or their baby's one hundredth day birthday party. There needs to be a policy on severance payments and levels of expenditure on entertainment.

3. **Encouraging Group Spirit**
   A culture of belonging should be developed, so staff can share common values and work to visible common objectives. Korean executives are likely to encourage this strongly as long as it doesn't prove too expensive! Company mottoes, staff picnics, hiking weekends and sports events can all assist. They will provide a golden opportunity for the foreigner to get to know his working colleagues at all levels in the company. Such events can be strenuous and alcoholic as Koreans like their playtime to be vigorous, enthusiastic and full of laughter. Singing will be mandatory at some part of the proceedings.

4. **Concise Communication**
   Critical attention needs to be paid to getting the point across so that it is properly understood. Repeat and repeat again is the best advice if in any doubt as to whether the real message has been grasped. The same is equally true in the reverse direction, where Koreans with limited English ability will go to painstaking lengths to communicate their point of view, only to back off at the crucial moment to avoid losing 'face' to an impatient foreigner.

5. **Promoting Non-Monetary Values**
   In this Confucian society, values such as status, title, 'face', recognition, group harmony and personal relationships are desperately important. Despite repeated emphasis on this subject, it is all too easily

forgotten when it really matters under the pressure of everyday office life.

6. **Delegation**
   Wise delegation which offers guidance and direction, but leaves much of the implementation to the local employees can yield surprisingly original results and solutions to problems. The outcome maybe very much the 'Korean way' but, after all, the company is operating in the Korean market, not in Europe or the USA.

7. **Being Patient**
   Arrogance is regarded as a common shortcoming of expatriate managers, particularly Americans. Patience coupled with a consistent and wise counselling approach is to be recommended. Koreans like to understand their partner and a firm but gentlemanly manner with a measure of genuine authority is likely to be well respected and warmly received.

8. **Training**
   The Koreans' desire for education extends into the workplace in the form of company 'training', but this doesn't necessarily follow 'needs for the job and career development training' associated with European and American companies. Training sessions may be held *en masse* and encompass all levels and professions within the company. Many are designed to develop staff into the appropriate culture, financial ideals and behaviour of the organisation.

   Often, group synergy and team spirit will be seen to take precedence over individual skills tuition. The foreign manager would be unwise to try and break with these traditions, but can use them as foundations upon which to build his own training modules associated with the skills needed by new technology and modern administration, developing the Korean system rather than working in opposition.

Foreign language training is likely to be seen as a long-term investment by the Korean partner. This can be realised both by formal college-type training and by informal in-house language discussion groups. Wives of foreign managers have sometimes led these groups in 'Use of Conversational and Colloquial English'. These can be lively and enjoyable sessions as well as being extremely useful and motivating. The Korean staff can then begin to understand visiting foreign dignitaries who will insist on using incomprehensible expressions such as 'talking through my hat' or 'off the top of my head'!

The foreign manager, therefore, has a real chance to combat the perceived view of some Koreans that the inward investors and multinationals are unsympathetic to the 'Korean way'. He can work to provide a warm and thriving environment for staff to perform to the best of their abilities and gain valuable development through new experiences, knowledge and skills. The process may also be very stimulating for the foreigner concerned and make his stay in Korea a lot more productive and considerably less stressful.

KOREAN EXECUTIVES REPRESENTING FOREIGN FIRMS

Globalisation of many multinational companies has led some to appoint Korean executives to represent their interests in their Korean firms and partnerships. This new trend is expected to accelerate during the next decade and is based on the premise that such people will be best able to increase business and market share by conforming with local business practices. Such executives, who may well have undergone extensive training in American or European business schools and their parent company's headquarters, often find themselves trapped between two opposing corporate cultures. There is a danger that this can lead to him being neither loved nor trusted by both his head office and his Korean employees. However, should he successfully bridge the cultural divide, the company may enjoy harmonious and rapid growth.

A foreign manager in Korea may well be pressed to search for, prepare and train a Korean executive to succeed himself at the end of his tour of duty. Such an exercise must be planned well in advance and involve open communication with all local staff and Korean partners. The rewards could be great but the risk element could be high unless rigorous selection and extensive training is exercised throughout.

8

Into Partnership

He who is really kind can never be unhappy
He who is really wise can never be confused
He who is really brave is never afraid

Confucius

SKIN-DEEP ADVERSITY

Some level of adversity exists in almost every foreign joint venture and business partnership in Korea, and occasionally it seems that common business objectives are all that remain to hold the relationship together. Conflict and potential communication breakdown due to cross-cultural differences lurk just skin-deep throughout corporate partnership-building, contract creation and every aspect of ongoing technology transfer, importation, production, advertising, financial control, administration and marketing. The list of flashpoints which can lead to traumatic problems is seemingly endless and experienced managers in Korea will probably feel that they have met them all! As a result, every working day in Korea can provide unique new experiences and troublesome adventures. These adventures can either raise blood pressure excessively or set adrenalin flowing with the excitement of challenge, largely dependent upon the foreign manager's aptitude to cope with cultural partner conflict and willingness to gain a sound understanding of Korean business etiquette.

COURTSHIP AND MARRIAGE

The first major difficulty in establishing a business relationship or joint venture in Korea is selecting the most suitable partner. Originally, it was thought that the large *Chaebol* conglomerates would make the most suitable spouses because of their depth of talent, access to capital and greater feel for the internationalisation process. They also tended to have a hot-line directly to the appropriate seats of influence within government. However, foreign companies discovered they did not always wish to join with an influential and powerful organisation. The policies of the large Korean partner did not necessarily meet the aims of the foreign company, and were likely to result in the venture being run in the tried and tested ways of the *Chaebol*, with little or no influence accepted from outside.

So it could be a handicap to join up with a *Chaebol* and many foreign companies have chosen instead to 'court' the medium and smaller firms within Korean industry. The government themselves have also encouraged such romance and it has become a popular approach.

A sensible prerequisite to any close liaison which may lead to marriage, is to research the partner. Having selected potential running mates, it is important to carefully check out the history and activities of all possible candidates. This should stretch beyond financial history and rate of growth towards analysis of its work ethic, attitudes of its chairman and directors, pay policies, staff turnover, comprehension of foreign languages, presence of labour unions, reputation with others in the industry, performance of its other joint ventures, if any, and interest in internationalisation. This cannot be achieved quickly, and if there is no representative office of the foreign company in Korea, it will take many visits to the country to winkle out all the relevant data. Employing the services of a local consultant in Korea can greatly assist this exercise and enhance the effectiveness of the results. This same consultant can begin to promote the personal contacts with key players in the organisations concerned, so exploratory meetings and dinners can be arranged. It may be a slow process, but if marriage is to be the end result, it's better the devil you know than the one you don't – and that applies to both sides! The marriage ahead is likely to be an affair of passionate views, lively debate, fiery disagreement, considerable stress and some hilarious moments. Through these multiple emotions, however, admiration and affection may grow. It will certainly be intense, as the Koreans will determinedly and frequently test the resolve of the foreigners to the limit and bring to the surface any hidden objectives which the overseas enterprise may have brought to their country.

The financial check on potential partners needs to command particular attention, as 'creative' accounting, to avoid showing losses at year end, is not unknown in Korea. The reasons for this are many, and include trying to show the company in the best possible light, to keep government enquiry firmly at arm's length and, of course, to save 'face'. The accounting mysteries may deepen further if the autocratic founder figure is still at the helm and is also a major shareholder in this and other companies in a complex empire. Thus local financial investigation and advice becomes essential in the pre-nuptial phase of any new venture. It must be conducted well in advance of the journey to the altar.

The wooing foreign consort can enhance his own chances for expediting these early steps by behaving openly, honestly, wisely and in a gentlemanly fashion during this 'getting to know you' period of friendship. He can invite and pay for senior Korean executives to visit his own company in Europe or USA to see facilities, standards of operation and meet the people – particularly the directors. The trip should be meticulously planned and include entertainment which may vary from a round of golf at a top club or a visit to the classiest show in town. Many Koreans are nervous away from their own country so support and encouragement will be needed. The agenda should include dinner at a good quality Korean restaurant (most major cities in Europe and USA have them), as they often miss their own cuisine. Chinese food can be used as a passable substitute. When Western food is served for the Korean guests, it is advisable to avoid lamb. It's not their favourite meat, and they find the smell very strong.

A successful and smooth running visit will encourage both partners to gain confidence with the people, the business and the dynamics involved in day-to-day management. A very personal approach with attention to detail and suitable farewell presents will reap benefits on return to Seoul or Pusan. The new potential partners will later be able to 'walk up the aisle' with a realistic feeling that despite cultural differences, the liaison will not end in divorce.

CONFLICT SOURCES

Assuming an essentially trouble-free courtship and honeymoon, sources of conflict between business or joint venture partners in Korea are many and varied. The global strategy of a multinational corporation may not be aligned to Korean business practice and even minor incompatibilities in personal or organisational objectives can potentially lead to severe strains in the relationship. The main purpose for the foreign company may be to gain a foothold in a potentially lucrative developing market and then return maximum profits back to the home country. The objective of the Korean company may centre on increasing market share, recording steady growth, maximising export potential and demonstrating a responsible contribution to the quality of life. Steering a safe passage between these conflicting goals is demanding upon both sides and it is advisable that at least some of the cards are laid upon the table from the outset. However, the wise foreigner will still have a few aces kept carefully up his sleeve to combat future difficulties and offer as a trade-off. Because of possible communication difficulties, the aims and objectives should be written in both languages.

Management control will almost certainly be challenged early in the life of a joint venture. This is because the Koreans almost invariably have responsibilities for day-to-day production, administration, financial and sales operations. Despite the new technology or product, they will see it as their market and act accordingly with their traditional management methods. This is likely to happen even if the original contract stipulates that the foreign partner has full responsibility for a key activity such as quality control. In these circumstances, the foreigner has to dig his heels in and firmly, but politely, show his resolve to stick with the words of the contract and the culture of his own company. Product quality responsibilities for newly transferred technology must always remain with the foreign partner. Although modern quality assurance concepts such as Total Quality Management (TQM) are beginning to be adopted, Koreans have a reputation for short-cutting in manufacturing operations to save money and to 'Koreanise' the product. If this situation is seen as a possibility, training the Korean staff in the advantages of operating with a rigid quality assurance programme must rate as top priority, and the cost advantages should be emphasised.

Lack of routine engineering maintenance is another area where operational efficiency and product quality may be threatened. Once again, the international drive towards demonstrable quality is pulling Korean industry forward into the benefits of routinely maintaining engineering equipment. However, it may not have yet reached all parts of the smaller companies, and the cost of introducing a maintenance system in terms of labour and spare parts could well be disputed. The foreigner is advised to prepare in advance and include appropriate text in both the contract and written aims and objectives of the manufacturing operation.

Any aspect of the business which involves upfront expenditure targeted to achieve longer term gains is likely to lead to debate and conflict, particularly at the beginning of the partnership or, in the case of the joint venture, the marriage. At this time, cash flows may be difficult and material/equipment transfer prices, inventory levels, product promotional advertising, selling practices and marketing techniques could be questioned in an attempt to save costs. Personnel activities, such as the annual salary increase and bonuses, may also lead to disagreement. Recruitment of staff of the relevant skills, knowledge and experience at the proper salary level can lead to surprising conflict. Korean executives can be tempted to recruit people too young and too inexperienced for the task, in order to cut back the revenue cost of salaries.

Thoughtless meddling with organisational structure is a sure-fire way to cause conflict. Organisational change may be necessary to successfully manage the enterprise but cannot be achieved without major discussion with the Korean executives at the highest level. All the aspects of social and business status must be considered, together with the age and experience of the staff in the organisation. This tricky subject may best be handled by planting the seed of the idea with the senior Korean staff and waiting for germination and response some weeks later. By this time, the various options will have been debated away from the ears of the foreigner and, with ordinary luck, a conclusion reached which will be to the satisfaction of both sides. Procedures for appointment of senior staff should be agreed by both sides in the original partnership arrangements. Mutual agreement during appointment of such key staff is an excellent way to cement harmonious relationships.

The Korean product market is presently being transformed by increased disposable income, rapid urbanisation, wider choice and an explosion of young consumers. Breaking into this potentially lucrative circumstance requires new expertise and yet another crossing of the cultural barrier. Western marketing methods may not suit the local situation and consumer market research has a short history. The incoming foreign marketing expert needs to work with considerable care and patience with his Korean colleagues to find the most suitable approach to product launch and advertising. Original concepts presented by foreigners can be greeted with distaste by local marketing expertise and proposals can even be taken as a personal affront – an indication of Korean incompetence. Conflict situations abound but rewards can be great. Around 60 per cent of Koreans regard themselves as middle-class and their behaviour patterns incline towards middle-class values and a diverse range of consumable products. A visit to the Lotte or Midopa department stores in Seoul on a Saturday afternoon will provide a vivid example of this trait. There is excellent marketing potential and, particularly amongst the young, a leaning towards Western-style and imported goods.

CONFLICT PREVENTION

Having established that conflict will be a constant and nagging potential feature of business in Korea, the astute foreigner will lay down a set of guidelines targeted to prevent conflict but still achieve corporate and personal objectives. Hard work, immense tolerance and superhuman patience can be regarded as 'given' requirements, but if the new manager applies the following, life in the office and progress with the partner will be eased:

1. **Agree Policies and Procedures**
   Establish simple and agreed partnership policies and procedures. Some may have been agreed during contract agreement but the actual business situation will probably have developed differently. Koreans will appreciate progression of the partnership in

such a way, as it is a sign of trust and a willingness to compromise to reach the best way forward. The foreign manager should always keep one eye on the original contract, however, lest he is encouraged to stray too far from the carefully created initial objectives.

2. **Anticipate Problems**
Although Koreans seem to have an insatiable capacity to surprise, particularly at the end of a busy day, conflicts can often be predicted by use of simple intelligence-gathering techniques over lunch and dinner, through walking the floor or through the skills of a good secretary.

3. **Keep Communication Channels Open**
Ensure personal communication channels are always kept open, even in the most stressful circumstances. Koreans may see it as a failure on their own part, as well as the foreigner's, if dialogue breaks down.

4. **Keep Records**
Keep meticulous records of all negotiations and business transactions. Good records management is an under-rated technique and a foreign manager should create systems which allow rapid and reliable search and retrieval. The records must include Korean translations of key documents and minutes of important meetings.

5. **Use Local Korean Skills**
Accept that the Korean partner has special knowledge of his own market and can apply hard-earned skills to the benefit of both in matters such as government negotiations, customer interface and staff welfare. Encourage him to use those skills and respect, rather than always question, his judgement. Foreigners don't always know best!

6. **Build Personal Relationships**
   Build a personal and harmonious relationship and constantly develop it over time. It will do much to build trust, confidence and a mutual understanding. Getting to know wives and families should be one aim, but not pushed too hard as some Koreans could regard this as an intrusion. Sharing hobbies and sporting interests is usually successful and the common pastimes could stretch from tennis, badminton, golf, ten-pin bowls and table tennis to fishing, hiking and backpacking.

7. **Manage Change**
   Be prepared to cope with and manage change. The change will arise from new and probably rapidly evolving business in this fast developing country which has experienced formidable growth. The new manager must adapt to rates of change far in excess of the norm in Europe and the USA, and it will exert pressure on both partners.

8. **Remember Confucius**
   Last but not least, always remember our friend Confucius. His spirit will be an all-pervading presence at every meeting and will influence almost all decisions made by the Koreans. He won't go away, so it's advisable to learn to live with him and maybe even occasionally enjoy the company of his far-reaching principles.

CONFLICT RESOLUTION

Assuming prevention techniques, no matter how brilliant, will fail from time to time, the foreign manager must be ready with methods by which conflicts can be resolved. Whenever possible they should be implemented early in the dispute, before tempers become frayed and emotions such as resentment and anger take too firm a hold. Many conflicts cannot be resolved immediately and both parties must be prepared to be patient, learn to understand the personalities involved and seek to gain longer term relationship benefits as a spin off from the eventual solution. Try to:

1. **Analyse the Reasons for the Conflict**
    They may not always be obvious and could have arisen from an unsuspecting attack on the Confucian principles which abound within the company. A few thoughtless words may have been spoken at the end of a tiresome day and the words may have been misinterpreted due to poor communication. The partner may, of course, be deliberately testing the foreign partner's resolve to stand by clauses in a contract or written agreement. If the analysis fails to provide the cause, as will frequently be the case, a few judicious questions to the most trusted junior colleagues may provide clues. This may best be achieved off site on neutral premises such as the snug bar in one of the major hotels.

2. **Avoid Western Logic**
    Having established at least a pointer to the difficulty, the next golden rule is to try and avoid using Western-style logic and problem-solving techniques to lead to an answer. Think Korean and find an emotional, abstract way to influence the Korean partner. Reference to the contract is unlikely to yield results and may further antagonise the people concerned.

3. **Be Pleasant**
    Always try to be approachable and go to great lengths to verify that, whatever the depth of the

conflict, personal relationships will not be under threat and maintenance of harmony is of paramount importance. This can be achieved by using personal skills and choosing appropriate places and surroundings for debate and discussion. The corner of a crowded noisy office is no place to conduct a serious debate. Much better to settle in a comfortable chair over a cup of ginseng tea, or go to a quiet bar or private room in a restaurant. Demonstration of a willingness to succeed is essential at all times.

4. **Compromise**
Be prepared to give and take to find a suitable compromise. In the heat of exchanges, it is sometimes difficult to understand that such compromises in Korea can actually benefit both sides and lead the venture positively forward. As mentioned earlier, the wise foreign manager will have anticipated conflict and have a number of offers ready for diplomatic negotiation. These might be financial, be associated with timing and quantity of technology transfer, a trade-off over transfer prices or even inventory levels. However, it is never advisable to compromise over product quality, no matter how much it may be threatened. As stated before, yielding on quality issues could be the start of a slippery slope downwards.

5. **Sleep on It**
When the going gets tough during the conflict and stress levels rise, it is better to call a break. This will probably be welcomed by all, as the problem rarely looks quite so daunting the following day and blood pressures will have declined to normal levels. An overnight break gives the foreign manager a chance not only to reflect in peace and quiet, but also to contact head office by phone or fax to share the

difficulty and lay a plan for continued debate, particularly if a strategic or financial trade-off may be required.

6. **Keep the Dialogue Flowing**
Many conflicts consist of a number of parts, interlinking to build up the whole issue of disagreement. Rather than hit the conflict head on and suffer equally stubborn and resistant opposition, dialogue can often be maintained harmoniously by nibbling away around the edges. Taking one bite at a time may not only speed up the meal but also improve the digestion! This gentle dialogue can be continued over many days if necessary and must never be rushed. It is perhaps worth emphasising again that the Korean partner may be super-sensitive over some loss of control in the business venture, and may constantly feel threatened that the foreigner wants to extract even more. In some cases, of course, he may be right in this assumption and it can lead to formidable barriers to progress.

7. **Keep it Confidential**
Bad news spreads quickly amongst the foreign community in Korea and there may be direct competitors to the venture dining on the next table at the Hilton, Hyatt, Shilla Hotels or in the Seoul Club. The business environment in Korea is difficult enough already without giving away chances of competitive advantage to others.

8. **Use a Mediator**
When patience, time and the will to succeed are running out, it may be the moment to call in a mediator, the same wise Korean who has helped investigate and negotiate the original partnership. This is possibly a face-loss situation for both sides, so is

often held as the last resort when all else has failed. He will need well briefing with the perceived root cause of the conflict and a list of potential trade-offs to be used to reach a satisfactory settlement.

Most conflicts will end amicably leaving both partners wiser and with a firmer bridge between the two cultures. A few minor skirmishes early within the business relationship might actually strengthen resolve to prevent conflict over major issues in the future. In extremely serious cases of conflict, where corporate communication is on the verge of breakdown, it could be necessary to bring in a senior executive from head office. It is a ploy to be used infrequently and should be handled tactfully so it is seen as an indication of the foreign company's sincere concern that a peaceful settlement must be generated. The personal meeting of the minds by the senior executives from both sides, often over dinner, can be the mechanism to create a solution in the most severe cases. It has even been suggested by the more cynical expatriates that the generation of the conflict was only a ploy to bring the senior executive to Korea after normal invitations had failed!

9
Enjoying Leisure

A distant journey ahead begins only when the first step has been taken.

Korean proverb

DISCOVERING KOREA

Sadly, Korea has never made the headlines as a primary Asian tourist destination, hence business visitors often fail to realise what a rich diversity of places there are to see and experience on this peninsula. Korea is a country with a splendid mountain landscape which vividly changes colour through the four seasons. Spring is heralded by yellow forsythia and the purple haze of azalea. The deep green of the summer months gives way to an autumn crescendo of red and gold which has people flocking in thousands to the country resorts. In winter, the white dusting of snow adds depth and height to the mountain scene. The people's love, almost obsession, with all things Korean has meant that their culture is freely on show for all to see, in the form of museums, temples and performing arts. One of the joys of visiting and living in Korea is to have the opportunity to explore and absorb some of this spectacular beauty and unique ancient tradition. The contrast between the hustle and bustle of Korea's main cities and the absolute peace of a temple in a wooded valley only a few miles away is truly amazing. Even the concrete jungle in Seoul has surprising havens of tranquility tucked away around street corners, particularly in the hilly northern part of the city. The country has much to offer and every visitor should take the opportunity to leave the hotel, pause awhile, take a deep breath, enjoy the constant attack on all five senses, then go forth to discover Korea!

The whole Korean peninsula is about 1000 km long and 200 km wide at its narrowest point. The land area is split approximately half and half between North and South. Approximately 70 per cent of South Korea is mountainous, particularly towards the east coast. To the south and west, the slopes descend slowly towards the coastal plains adjacent to the Yellow Sea, where the bulk of Korea's agricultural and rice crops are grown. The Demilitarised Zone (DMZ) at the 38th Parallel divides North from South. Around 25 per cent of South Korea's population of 43 million lives in Seoul. Administratively, the country is divided into nine provinces and one special city, Seoul. Other major cities are Pusan, Inchon, Taejon, Kwangju and Taegu.

Korea's climate is temperate and has four distinct seasons, all of which are more reliable than the weather of Western Europe. Spring is underway by early April as the first blossoms come into flower. The cherry is a particular favourite. By June, the weather has warmed considerably and the monsoon arrives around the end of the month. July can be very wet and the period until mid-August very hot with temperatures into the low 30s°C. Autumn is Korea's favourite season as the weather cools and the skies become a heavenly clear blue. There are a number of public holidays and festivals at this time. Winter arrives in December and can bring periods of intense cold, dry weather with temperatures dropping as low as $-20°C$ if the wind turns to the North from Siberia. Snowfall is not usually heavy except in the mountain areas, where ski resorts are strategically placed. It is an invigorating climate and the best months to visit are probably May, September and October.

Travel is relatively easy. Once the basic network of roads and bridges in Seoul is understood, driving is not too daunting. It's largely every man for himself and the foreigner must be prepared to act defensively behind the wheel! The taxi service is generally good. Although Korean taxi drivers have a reputation of being rude, most foreigners have few problems other than finding themselves unexpectedly sharing their cab with a Korean family. Taxi drivers' understanding of foreign language is limited so it is often best to have destinations written in Korean beforehand. Seoul's subway is clean, reliable, easy to use but best avoided in the rush hour.

Travelling further afield can be achieved without undue problems by car and the train service is fast and comfortable. Korea's air network is good and is strongly recommended to take the visitor to the island of Cheju. The long-distance bus network is always busy and is a cheap way to travel. Regular organised tours from half a day in Seoul, up to twelve days taking in the most spectacular tourist sights, can easily be arranged via hotels and travel agents. There is plenty of good quality tourist literature available, and a camera is a must on even the briefest of trips to a street market or ancient palace.

SEOUL

Seoul is more than just the capital of the nation; it is the thriving heart of the Republic of Korea, and has a magnetic pull on all residents of the country. This sprawling conurbation has expanded rapidly in the last fifteen years, particularly south of the River Han, where new apartments and shopping areas are geometrically laid out and criss-crossed with wide streets and pavements. Most of Seoul's interest lies to the north of the river around the striking Nam-san, a tree-clad hill which dominates the horizon, at least partially due to the huge tower on its summit. Exploration is best started in this area and most points can be reached easily using the hotel shuttle buses which ply a circular route throughout the day.

Downtown

There is no better place to start discovering Seoul than in City Hall Plaza. Considered by many to be the very epicentre of the City, it has the Plaza Hotel on its south side, City Hall on the north, Toksu Palace to the west and a wall of fuming traffic circulating around its centre. Armed with a Seoul map which is obtainable at the hotel, the visitor can head north up Sejong-no, having first used the pedestrian subway system and discovered the vast network of underground routes and shopping arcades – the city beneath. The statue of Korea's naval commander Admiral Yi Sun-Shin dominates Sejong-no but, noticeable on the left, is the red brick Anglican Cathedral close to the British Embassy. Further along the wide boulevard is the huge modern Sejong Cultural Centre which is almost directly opposite the American Embassy, and is used for concerts and conferences. Beyond the ancient Kwanghwamun Gate, at the end of Sejong-no, is the National Museum. This large building dates back to the 1920s and is the home for thousands of priceless items from Korean history. It is an excellent place to begin to feel the pulse of Korea's cultural past.

Returning back down the same broad highway, a left turn can be made after the American Embassy to visit the antique shops in Insa-dong, which has the nickname of 'Mary's Alley'. Here one can browse to one's heart's content amongst art and handicrafts. It's difficult to leave without purchasing something. Nearby lies Chogye-sa, the main Buddhist temple in Seoul. Whilst certainly not the most attractive temple around the city, it is an important centre of Korean Buddhism and the focal point of celebration on Buddha's birthday each year.

If the visitor still has energy and time remaining, a return can be made to City Plaza before moving towards Myong-dong which is the fashion centre of Seoul. It has chic and high priced clothes shops where international styles as well as Korean fashions are available. At night time, Myong-dong starts swinging as the alleyways transform to an important centre of entertainment for the city's jet-set. Some of Seoul's prime hotels are nearby, as are the most modern and large department stores. A visit to the Lotte or Midopa Stores should be on everyone's agenda. The range of goods is high but so is the price. The Lotte is the nearest Korean equivalent to Harrods. Finally in this tour of downtown Seoul, the Myong-dong Catholic Cathedral is worthy of mention. It is perched on a small hill and became an important focal point for demonstrations during the people's push for greater democracy in 1987.

Palaces

Seoul's palaces draw visitors and Koreans alike, not only because of their interest and beauty, but also because they have wide open spaces where families can picnic and children can play. Seoul is very short on parks and palace grounds act as substitutes. The palaces are all central, easily accessible to the visitor and tours can be arranged through the major hotels. Toksu Palace's gate faces City Hall Plaza and the complex of buildings was constructed at the end of the fifteenth century. It is here that King Kojong lived in his retirement until he died in 1919 having watched his country annexed by the Japanese. Hence the palace had a significant role at the sad finish to the Yi Dynasty. A statue of the great King Sejong stands in the grounds, often surrounded by parents or teachers telling children of the important contributions he made to Korea's history.

Rather more interesting is Kyongbok Palace situated behind the National Museum at the end of Sejong-no. The large grounds of the palace are a particular favourite for Korean schoolchildren who, armed with paintbrushes and easels, try and depict some of the scenic splendour. Kyongbok is lovely in all seasons and is the perfect place to 'people watch' and observe Koreans at leisure. During the week it is generally peaceful, but at the weekend is packed with noisy, cheerful families carrying picnics and cameras. Kyongbok was built in the fourteenth century but has been reconstructed many times as a result of fire. Perhaps the most charming of the buildings in the Palace is the diminutive Hyangwan pavilion, picturesquely situated in the centre of a lotus pond. It is perfect in July when the blossoms can be admired.

Just to the east lies most visitors' favourite place in Seoul, the Changdok Palace. Originally dating back to the fifteenth century, it was the official residence of many kings of the Yi Dynasty up to Sunjong, the last, until he died in 1926. It is a well-preserved palace, and behind it lies Piwon, the Secret Garden, so called because it was used as a private park and pleasure ground by the Royal Family. The Palace and Piwon can only be visited on organised guided tours and the exquisite Piwon provides a myriad of photo-opportunities with its lovely pavilions connected by bridges over small streams amongst the trees. It is worth a visit in all four seasons and perfect for a peaceful hour or two when the stress, noise and pace of city life weighs heavily upon the shoulders!

As an encore and to complete the set of Seoul's central royal residences, Changgyong Palace lies just to the north east of Piwon, and across the road is the Chongmyo Royal Shrine, the last resting place of the Choson kings and queens. It is here in early May that the shrine buildings are open to the public for the annual Confucian ceremony mentioned in Chapter 4. This colourful and solemn occasion is also an opportunity to hear original court music played, whilst respects and offerings are made to the ancient spirits within the shrine.

Yoido

A visit to Yoido can provide a complete contrast to the shops and palaces of the downtown area. Yoido has, perhaps rather generously, been called the Manhattan of Seoul.

It contains the city's financial centre and is home to the Korean Stock Exchange. It is dominated by the enormous Yoido Plaza where one can pedal away frustrations on a hired bike in a traffic-free zone – a great chance to behave childishly amongst hundreds of others doing the same. On one side of the Plaza lies the Korean War Museum, which is a grim reminder of events of the past with a good display of the armoury used in the conflict. Towards one end of Yoido island is the National Assembly and nearby is the Full Gospel Central Church, one of the largest churches in the world. Totally dominating the whole of Yoido is the Daehan Building. With sixty-three floors, it is one of Asia's tallest and most graceful buildings. It is a tourist attraction in its own right, with an observation deck, IMAX theatre, shops and an excellent aquarium, making it great fun for the family.

Down the River

Seoul's River Han doesn't have much traffic, but pleasure boats do ply the waterway between Yoido and the Olympic Complex to the east. It is worth making this cruise to get an overall view of the city and to sit at close quarters amongst Koreans at play. Much of the strip along the banks of the river has now been transformed into green parks with sports facilities but the immediate backdrop of endless concrete apartments is very unattractive. The boat stops near the Seoul Sports Complex, which houses the graceful Olympic Stadium, whose shape was based upon the curvature of a Choson-period ceramic vessel. The stadium is open to the public and has a Visitor Centre describing all the sports facilities available within the complex.

This part of Seoul is very much a growth area with an explosion of new apartments and shops. Departmental stores here rival those in downtown and can be a lot cheaper. Traffic moves more freely and there are less choking exhaust fumes. Nearby lies Lotte World, an enormous indoor leisure centre. As well as containing a top-class hotel, it has a shopping mall, folk centre and theme park. The folk centre gives the visitor an opportunity to see craftsmen display their skills. The indoor theme park has modern rides and, as an educational attraction, street scenes from around the world. It is linked to an outdoor 'Magic Island' theme park surrounded by a lake. They are all wonderful spots to observe and begin to understand the Korean people.

Two other places should be on the foreigner's list to visit as soon as possible after arriving in Seoul. Nam-san (South Mountain) rises as a green cone amongst the urban sprawl. It's possible to drive to the top or take a cable car. Much better, however, is to walk up to the summit through the gardens and recreational area near the Hilton Hotel. It is here that elderly Koreans gather to talk and enjoy their retirement, and can be seen wearing traditional linen costume in summer. Steps take the visitors upwards to a small recreational area and viewpoint and, as they pause for breath, they should spare a thought for the Korean gentleman who walked on his hands up the whole route. Korea has its eccentrics too! It would be a shame to walk all this way without taking the lift to the top of Nam-san Tower and it is worth a few Won to take the trip. The circular viewing gallery gives a spectacular view of the whole of Seoul, a vista which is equally good at nighttime. It's the best way to learn the geography of the city. After a visit to Nam-san itself, an enjoyable way to spend an evening is at Korea House, which lies at the foot of its Northern slopes. Korea House is unashamedly a very good tourist trap. Inside a building of traditional architecture, Korean food is served in dining rooms large and small, and it is an opportunity to taste and try some of the mouthwatering and fiery dishes. An added feature is the performance of traditional Korean music and dance in a comfortable small theatre within the complex. Top-rated performers give a very colourful show.

Shopping

A wide variety of merchandise can be bought in Seoul and the foreigner's first stop is usually Itaewon, which caters very well for the Western tourist. The main street is lined with clothing shops and stalls selling everything from T shirts to ski suits. Quality is generally good but it is worth shopping around to find the best bargains as they may be in small stores buried down side streets or in basements. Custom-made suits can be obtained cheaply and reliably at any one of a hundred tailor shops. Once again, the most competitive prices are likely to be found away from the main street. Itaewon is a fun place to shop and is good for Korean souvenirs such as eel-skin products, ceramic ware, brassware, embroidery, leather goods, lacquerware and jewellery. Jade, amethyst and smoky topaz are three semi-precious minerals which continually catch the eye. Furs are one of the latest of Korea's shopping attractions.

The Korean shopkeepers and stallholders are invariably friendly. They enjoy haggling over price and giving service with a smile. A pair of jeans can be altered while you wait. When the feet tire, there are plenty of international fast food outlets to stock up an empty stomach and replenish energy levels. Itaewon also has supermarkets which stock food suitably packed and presented for foreigners and a number of specialist food shops and restaurants which serve European-style fare. This can be very welcome after an endless stream of garlic-dominated Korean business dinners.

Unfortunately for many, shopping begins and ends in Itaewon, perhaps because it is easy to reach and many of the shopkeepers speak some English. As soon as possible, visitors should take in the scents, sounds and sights of the Namdaemun, close to Seoul's ancient South Gate. Here one can buy almost anything within the maze of alleyways, shops and much larger multi-floored buildings. It's very entrepreneurial and totally fascinating to see the range of oriental goods on display. There aren't many foreign languages spoken, but by gesticulation, frantic arm waving and a lot of smiling, communication is easily possible and excellent deals can be struck. The deal may include a cup of coffee in return for a quick lesson in English conversation. As well as some bargain buys, there are superb scenes for the photographer and it is worth the effort to seek out the flower-market for dazzling colour and fascinating flower arrangements.

Having mastered the intricacies of Namdaemun, the newcomer to Seoul should then head for Tongdaemun, or the East Gate market. It is the largest and unquestionably the most striking market-place in Korea, if not Asia. Within this enormous area, one may see anything from live snakes and turtles, to brilliantly coloured silks, to stalls specialising in ginseng, electrical goods and seasonal fruits. There are shops selling household goods, sports equipment, furniture, clothing and bedding. There is even an area which concentrates on Chinese herbal medicine and acupuncture. Becoming blissfully lost in Tongdaemun is the perfect way to become intimately involved in Korea.

Rather more specialist and higher-priced shopping can be found in Myong-dong fashion centre amongst the many boutiques and within the Insa-dong artists and antique area, both mentioned earlier. Highest quality goods are available and Insa-dong, in particular, can yield some wonderful paintings, ceramics and exquisite Korean period furniture. Korean department stores lack the fun and excitement of street shopping but they do tend to deliver a more reliable level of quality and at a fixed price.

Best buys in Korea are largely a matter of taste, but reproduction antiques, ceramics and inlaid lacquerware are very popular. There is a word of caution, however, regarding counterfeit goods and imitation designer labels. There is plenty about and much of it is well disguised enough to fool the unwary. It's wise to ask for and keep receipts of any significant purchase.

Night Life

There is plenty of night-life to choose from in all of Korea's major cities. Many of the major hotels have night clubs and discotheques, but like elsewhere in the world they are stereotyped and plastic. The Yong-dong and Itaewon areas offer more variety and the latter tends to cater for foreign clientele. Such Korean night clubs can be good fun and are best visited with Korean colleagues who will pick the best, or those with the finest floor shows, music, hostesses, beverages and food. A foreigner amidst Koreans in a night club may well draw the attention of the stand-up comedians. If it occurs, sit back and enjoy the hilarity that will abound at your expense.

Gamblers are catered for in hotels in Seoul, Pusan, Kyongju and Chejudo, and details can be obtained on arrival. First-rate facilities can be found, including poker, blackjack and roulette. Some, of course, were built with American and Japanese tourists in mind.

Should the visitor want to 'go native' there are plenty of opportunities. Korean colleagues will no doubt introduce their guest to the Kisaeng Houses and Salon Bars together with the resident female companions. There are also Korean-style bars and beer halls where the late night reveller can drink local beer or *Makkoli* (brewed from rice) or *So-ju* (distilled from potatoes). He can also join in the singing and inevitable Karaoke. They are hot, noisy places where Koreans dispose of their work-a-day frustrations. The final calling place for the determined boozer is a tent pitched alongside one of the roads, where the last late night drinks and Korean food delicacies may be purchased.

A gentler evening may be had in one of the theatre restaurants or tourist Korean eating houses. There are many to choose from and they welcome Western wives and girlfriends. The food can be excellent and is best described as 'slightly Westernised Korean'. Music and a quality floor show can add an enjoyable touch to the evening and will be an introduction to traditional Korean music and dancing.

SEOUL OUTINGS

The first stop out of Seoul for visitors to Korea should be the Korean Folk Village, which lies to the south of the city, just off the Kyongbu Expressway. Easy to get to by coach or by car, the Folk Village offers an excellent view into Korea's past and is a thoroughly professional tourist attraction. It is worth spending a full and leisurely day wandering amongst period farmhouses and buildings of the past designed for rich, poor and nobility. There is a fully functioning group of weavers, blacksmiths, potters and others with handed down craft skills, and much of their produce is for sale. The restaurants sell the best of Korean food and the pancakes, in particular, are quite mouth-watering. Folk dancing and various musical events take place throughout the day.

Should any children in the party become bored with all the traditional Korean displays, and the noise of the folk music can induce headaches, nearby Yong-in Farmland might be the answer. It has an African-type safari and also a zoo, a small amusement park and a 'Global Village' which features cultural tableaux from around the world. Youngsters will enjoy the boat trip past figures and scenes from each country. Adults may well view the exhibits with a smile and a comment that 'only the Koreans could produce something like this!'

A more expansive zoo also lies to the south of the city, at Seoul Grand Park near a suburb called Kwachon. It is a major attraction and justly popular with Korean families at weekends. This popularity means that if a quiet visit is required in the company of small children, a weekday is infinitely preferable. Otherwise there will be a lot of pushing and shoving to see the premier exhibits.

Those people interested in celadon should definitely put Ichon on the itinerary. A simple journey by expressway to the south west of Seoul brings the tourist to the region where the brilliant Choson Dynasty white porcelain was made. The area around Ichon is littered with kilns belonging to Korea's most noted potters. Visitors not only see the production of the pots first-hand but also have the chance to purchase some of the finest quality celadon and porcelain direct from the potter. There are superb pieces for sale at lower prices than can be found in city centre shops.

A favourite excursion for lovers of mountains and lakes is to take the highway to Chunchon and discover the exquisite countryside of the North Han river. Possibilities include the island resort of Namisom in the centre of the river or further north to Chunchon itself, which is conveniently placed as a tourist resort for those who live in Seoul. Swimming, sailing, water-skiing and fishing are some of the sporting possibilities on the blue waters of lovely Chunchon lake. Even better is to travel further to Soyang Dam which has created an outstandingly beautiful lake. Here the tourist can either take a short boat trip across Soyang's tranquil waters and visit a fish farm or embark on a longer tour heading east on this magnificent waterway. Those with a day or two to spare can cruise on towards the Sorak mountains. Walking trails are available in all these areas and often lead to small Buddhist temples beautifully situated on tranquil mountainsides.

Opportunities for more serious hiking abound quite close to Seoul. At weekends, Korean families throng the trails to the more popular spots and in all weathers the picnic is very much in evidence. Picnics are taken very seriously and a splendid spread of food and drink will be produced. This is one of the rare occasions that the Korean male can be seen cooking as he becomes master of the barbecue. The day can become very alcoholic and, by afternoon, all thoughts of mountain climbing evaporate in favour of drinking and singing. Two of the most favoured walking areas are around Namhansansong Fortress to the south of Seoul, and Pukansansong Fortress on the northern boundary of the original ancient city.

More serious mountaineering and scrambling can be found on Pukan-san Mountain itself and nearby Tobong-san. The views from these lofty peaks are quite superb, but involve a full day's outing. For those unwilling to toil up the steepest slopes, a walk up Kwanak-san, the jagged ridge south of the river, is quite excellent. There is a picturesque temple on the route up from the south side and a tiny shrine right at the summit, which commands a panoramic view of the whole city.

The trip to Panmunjon inside the Demilitarised Zone is available by coach from the major hotels. It was the site of the armistice negotiations which ended the Korean War and has since been a place of ongoing peace talks, a sort of safety-valve to try and prevent recurring conflict between North and South. The route is quite short and follows Unification Highway directly north, crossing Freedom Bridge to arrive at the truce camp. It is a bizarre journey but extremely interesting and visitors are escorted by military personnel to Freedom House and a view into North Korea. Stories of border incidents are told and there is a chance to visit the Conference Room in the Joint Security Area, the place where routine dialogue between the two Koreas takes place. Some trips also take in one of the tunnels dug by the North Koreans under the DMZ and into the South. This was discovered by alert military personnel and the visitor can walk down directly into the tunnel itself. A day out in Panmunjon is a forceful reminder of the tension on the peninsula and gives an insight to some of the fears and hopes that lie inside every Korean citizen.

A full day excursion that should be high on everyone's list is the drive to Kanghwado, an island about 50 km north west of Seoul. It is reached across a narrow causeway and is perched on the estuary of the Han and Imjin rivers close to North Korea. The military are much in evidence in this part of the country. Kanghwado has much to offer the tourist and its soil favours the cultivation of the Ginseng root. The main magnet for visitors to the island is the 500 metre climb up Mani-san to the site of Tangun's altar at the summit of the mountain. It is an opportunity to look at a fabulous view on a clear day and also feel a part of historic Korean legend. Another way to travel back in time is to call in at Chondung-sa Temple, one of the oldest in Korea. The architecture is superb and in the temple grounds is a huge iron bell which is said to have been cast in the eleventh century in the Chinese style. It is designated a national treasure. Kanghwa town itself is home to a number of craft shops and lends itself to a leisurely stroll on a warm summer afternoon.

EASTERN KOREA

The Yongdong Expressway connects Seoul to the scenic Korean east coast and the combination of both mountains and beaches make this part of the country a favourite for summer vacations. Korean colleagues will insist that the first port of call for any foreign visitor taking a short break should be Sorak-san National Park. It can be found north of the coastal city of Kangnung and is about five hours drive from Seoul. This 'Snow Peak Mountain' is actually a collection of superb peaks and valleys and justly deserves all the praise heaped upon it by Korean outdoor enthusiasts. As it also has some Western-style hotels, it is ideal to enjoy a few days of beautiful countryside and fresh air. There are dozens of hiking trails to suit all levels of fitness and autumn is the prime time to make the journey as the colours are outstanding. At this time of year, a weekend is perhaps best avoided as veritable armies of Koreans descend upon the National Park. They travel overnight and burst upon the peaceful scene at the crack of dawn with fitness routines and joyful singing!

The east coast's other major attraction for foreigners is the Yongpyeong Ski Resort just off the Yongdong Expressway and to the south of the Odae-san National Park. It is a well equipped resort and receives more snow than the more inferior resorts nearer to Seoul. It has chair lifts and probably offers the best skiing in Korea although the season is a little short. Yongpyeong or 'Dragon Valley' as it is often known, is the venue for the 'Foreigners' Ski Weekend', a major social event on the expatriate calendar.

CENTRAL KOREA

The central part of Korea is sometimes overlooked as a tourist destination as people speed south or east. However, it is not without interest and has rugged and attractive mountains. A stop at the Independence Hall of Korea near Chonan can be made *en route*. It commemorates those who fought for Korea's freedom against the many foreign invasions during its history. However, Songni-san National Park is the focal point of this part of Korea. It is another beautiful area to visit and can be less crowded than Sorak-san. One of its main attractions is the splended Popchu-sa Temple, a large complex which includes a huge and much photographed bronze statue of Buddha. Songni-san can be used as a suitable base to explore and visit other National Parks in the area and the huge Chungju reservoir which offers a range of water sports and tourist attractions along its 50 km-long waterway.

SOUTH EAST KOREA

This part of the country has many superb tourist attractions, so those foreigners based in Pusan have the opportunity to study Korea's rich national heritage closely.

Kyongju was the capital of the Silla Kingdom for a thousand years and during this time became one of the world's major cultural centres. It is truly an open-air museum, with a wealth of history in and around the city. As a result, major hotels have sprung up in the Pomun Lake Resort area which cater admirably for Western needs. Tourist literature describes Kyongju's many attractions in detail, but it is worth highlighting the four principal gems. Firstly the Kyongju National Museum which houses some brilliant artifacts from Silla's past including gold crowns and the enormous 23 tonne Emille Bell. Nearby is the unique Tumuli Park which has a large collection of royal tombs. The famous 'Flying Horse' Tomb was excavated in 1974 and is open for viewing. It yielded thousands of treasures including a magnificent gold foil crown, a solid gold belt girdle and gold and jade tiger claw earrings.

The third major place of interest is east of Kyongju and is Pulguk-sa, Korea's most famous temple. It is in a wonderful setting and has been splendidly restored. The view up the front steps is one of the most photographed in the nation and a stroll amongst the sprawling complex will keep the camera shutter very busy. The fourth Kyongju gem, and many people's favourite, is the Sokkuram stone cave hermitage up in the mountains near Pulguk-sa. It is easily accessible along a winding road and is a charming grotto set amongst the trees on the mountainside which contains a granite Buddha image. This serene statue is said by many experts to be the most perfect Buddha of its kind anywhere in the world.

Pusan is Korea's second largest city and the main port for ferry services to Japan. Its most infamous scenic attraction is the local beach which seems to feature every August in Korean newspapers with pictures of up to half a million people crammed together like ants enjoying sand and sea! The city has excellent hotels and good shopping areas. The United Nations Cemetery has an attractive setting and is the final resting place of many UN soldiers who fell in the Korean War.

Other attractions in this part of Korea include Haein-sa Temple, which houses the 80,000 wooden printing blocks that make up the Tripitaka Koreana and are the basis of the most important editions of Buddhist literature. Also, the Hallyosudo Waterway running to the south and west of Pusan. It is a picturesque marine park and it was in these waters that the legendary Admiral Yi defeated the Japanese with his turtle ships.

SOUTH WEST KOREA

The least visited part of Korea is the south west corner, a portion of the country which is centred on the city of Kwangju. It is an area of fertile rice paddies and jagged coastline. Chindo island, which gives its name to the most common breed of dog in Korea, is probably the most famous tourist destination. Here, the so-called 'Moses Miracle' takes place twice a year when the spring tides reveal a land bridge between Chindo and a small neighbouring island. Thousands walk across the narrow strip of solid ground.

Chiri-san National Park is a great favourite with discerning Korean hikers and many prefer it to Sorak-san. It contains some of the highest peaks in the land and is noted for its brilliant autumn foliage. Buddhist temple specialists will also find Chiri-san full of interest as there are many buildings tucked away in the lush green valleys. Tea was first brought to Korea from China in Silla times and cultivated here on the slopes of Chiri-san's peaks. Some of the tea plants still grow wild today in this area.

CHEJU – ISLAND OF THE GODS

This isolated southern outpost of South Korea is volcanic in origin and hence unlike any other landscape within the

Republic. Mount Halla-san, the tallest point in the country at 1950 m, is a long extinct volcano and dominates the island. The pace of life here in Cheju is slower than elsewhere and the climate is moist, warm and windy. The fields are fertile and there are quaint villages with houses built from the dark volcanic lava rock. There are sandy beaches, natural tourist attractions and good hotels. No wonder Cheju is the favourite destination for young honeymooners and it is easily accessibly by air from Korea's major cities.

Foreigners spending time in Korea would do well to come over to Cheju and linger awhile. The people are friendly and there is plenty to see and do at a leisurely pace. A few days here can relieve the stress of a testing business relationship and soothe the most shattered nerve ends. Visitors stay at either Cheju City in the north of the island or at the Chungmun Resort Complex in the south. The many tourist attractions can be conveniently visited by hiring a self-drive car or car with guide. The latter may be more expensive, but the guide will know exactly where to go and the best restaurants *en route*. However, in true Korean style, he will expect to take pictures of you in front of every single attraction on the way!

The island boasts fine folklore museums, picturesque waterfalls, caves and one of the longest lava tubes in the world, a staggering 10 km of inky blackness. Cheju has volcanic cones and craters, hiking trails to lofty Halla-san, women who dive for shellfish, fascinating local architecture, bananas, oranges and the strange Tolharubang statues. These stone grandfathers are made from black lava and used to be considered as guardian deities. They crop up all over Cheju and miniature versions of this phallic gentleman can be bought as souvenirs.

Most people enthuse over Cheju and it justly earns its reputation as an excellent holiday spot. Even botanists find plenty to interest them as in the sheltered hollows on the south coast some sub-tropical plants grow at their most northern latitude. Except when occasional typhoons pass through, it is an idyllic destination and all visitors should be prepared to stay a few extra days and buy plenty of film for the camera. This island is really rather special.

ROYAL ASIATIC SOCIETY

One way to learn more about Korea's culture and travel to the most interesting parts of the country is to join the Korea Branch of the Royal Asiatic Society (RAS). It was founded in 1900 by foreigners living in Seoul and is now a thriving non-profit-making organisation providing fascinating information about the 'Land of the Morning Calm'. The RAS develops understanding of Korea through tours attended by people who want to learn about the country in an informal relaxed manner. These may stretch from one end of the country to the other, be a half-day picnic in a forgotten fortress or a full weekend tour taking in a picturesque island. The trips can involve boat rides, mountain climbing or visit a traditional paper-making or brassware factory. There is something for everybody.

The tours are backed up by semi-monthly meetings where Korean and Western speakers share their experiences and talk authoritatively on a wide range of topics associated with the geography, natural history, dance, music, arts and drama of the country. Also the RAS publish Annual Transactions of the Society, which are considered to be one of the foremost sources of scholarly information on Korea. From the mid 1960s a book publishing programme was launched which now features over two hundred titles. Many can be purchased from the Society's Korea branch office and provide a wonderful additional way to discover Korea. The contact address for the RAS is in Chapter 10.

10
Korean Fact File

Sprays of wheat stalk bend lower if grains are solid
Likewise the more knowledge we have, the more we feel inadequate.

Korean proverb

CONSTITUTION AND GOVERNMENT

The Republic of Korea's Constitution was created in 1948 and then amended in 1987. It guarantees all citizens equality before the law, personal freedom, basic human rights and participation in government. Amendments to the Constitution can be made by referendum.

The president has executive authority, is the head of State for foreign affairs, the head of the executive branch for domestic affairs and the Commander-in-Chief of the armed forces. He has a five-year term of office and cannot be re-elected. The president administers via the State Council, which he chairs, and is assisted by the prime minister who is Vice Chairman. This Council is a decision- and policy-making forum. Legislative power is exercised by a single chamber National Assembly. Two-thirds of its seats are occupied by members elected by direct popular vote, and the remainder divided amongst members of the various political parties in proportion to the seats won by the direct election. National Assembly responsibilities include ratification of foreign treaties, the budget, and approval of legislative bills.

POPULATION

South Korea's population is about 43 million with a growth rate of around 1 per cent. It is a 'young' country as about 50 per cent of the residents are under 25 years of age. The population has become increasingly urbanised and the farming community now only accounts for about 20 per cent of the total labour force, a figure which has halved in the last fifteen years or so.

ENTRY POINTS

The main entry point is Seoul's Kimpo Airport a few miles west of the city. Pusan and Chejudo also have international airports although the latter is mainly for tourist trade. The principal international destination is Tokyo but there are frequent flights to Hong Kong, other main Asian cities, the USA and Western Europe. There are many good quality ports for shipping, but the most important are Pusan and Inchon, both of which have container terminals.

COMMUNICATION

Korea has direct dialling throughout and an extensive telephone network as can be seen by the frequency with which people are seen with a telephone receiver in their hand! Associated telex and fax systems can be quickly installed and there are few problems with transmission of data. The mail service is reliable although business addresses in city centres are likely to receive faster delivery than residential areas further afield. Courier services are available for critical items.

SEOUL – THE HEAD OFFICE

Around a quarter of Korea's population lives in Seoul, and as the capital city, it has many of the government's administrative offices. In recent years, some of these have been moved away from the centre, to the south of the River Han. Most major Korean companies have their head offices in Seoul and this enormous city is unquestionably the hub of the nation. It has the most important universities and the major theatres and entertainment facilities. Leading international music and drama groups are frequent visitors and their performances are well patronised by a discerning Korean people. They appreciate top-class music and arts from other nations as well as their own. All this makes Seoul a most satisfying environment in which to visit and work, where communication is good and business contacts are geographically close at hand.

ENTRY REQUIREMENTS

Foreigners visiting Korea must have a current passport and entry visa unless the stay is for less than fifteen days. A visa can be obtained from the Korean consulate and its duration is ninety days. It is not normally renewable. A long term visa needs sponsorship, usually by a company in Korea, together with evidence of employment. On arrival in the Republic, the foreigner who wishes to become resident must apply for a residence certificate within sixty days at the appropriate District Immigration Office. Those holding a residence certificate who leave and then return must obtain a re-entry permit from the District Immigration Office.

HOUSING

Good quality housing is readily available, and Seoul in particular, has ample choice of apartments and detached houses. Accommodation is expensive and even the most modest apartment will cost in excess of $2,500 per month, with houses at up to three times that figure – maybe more if a fashionable district is chosen. This cost can seem quite exorbitant if the rent for the entire letting period is required in advance as is often the case.

SCHOOLS

Schooling for foreign children is not a problem and information on schools in which English, French or German are the main languages can readily be obtained from Foreign Embassies. Seoul Foreign School can be highly recommended and takes students up to the age of eighteen and International Baccalaureate level. Many of these schools have highly qualified and dedicated teachers who perform to excellent standards of scholarship and discipline.

CURRENCY

The Republic of Korea currency is the Won. Bank note denominations are W10,000, W5,000 and W1,000. Coin denominations are W500, W100, W50, W10, W5 and W1. Traveller's cheques and foreign bank notes can be converted into Won at foreign exchange banks and authorized money changers, and the exchange rate is subject to the usual market fluctuations. A typical rate against the US dollar in 1993 would be W750–800. The usual major international credit cards are accepted at large hotels, major department stores and tourist restaurants. In small businesses and shops, however, cash remains king and those who do accept credit cards may charge a handling fee.

HEALTH CARE

Reasonable health care is available for foreigners and most use international clinics either privately run or as part of large general hospitals such as 'Severance'. Details can be obtained from Foreign Embassies. Pharmaceutical products and cosmetics are freely available. In fact a walk around a major city shows that there are pharmacies on almost every corner. Here, Korean-made and a few imported drugs are dispensed by the resident pharmacist. He will even dispense a single aspirin tablet for an immediate headache. These small shops often do excellent business in the early morning selling small bottles of tonics and pick-me-ups to Korean businessmen 'hungover' from the excesses of an evening on the *So-ju*! Locally manufactured drugs should be considered safe and effective.

NEWSPAPERS

There are two English language daily newspapers, *The Korea Times* and *The Korea Herald*. These are published daily, except Mondays. They provide a good overview of local politics and events, together with items of major world news and sport. There are a number of English language economic and business journals. Perhaps the most popular are *Korea Business World* and *Business Korea*. Some international newspapers and magazines can be purchased at major hotel bookstores.

LANGUAGE

The Korean language, which is independent from Chinese and Japanese, is part of the altaic group of languages which includes Korean, Hungarian, Mongolian and Finnish. The Korean language is formed from an alphabet called *Hangul* which has ten vowels and fourteen consonants. It is phonetic in form, not pictorial. Various combinations of these make up approximately fifty-four sounds or syllables. Despite having their own independent language, Koreans can read up to over 1,800 Chinese characters, due to the long historical links between China and Korea.

For foreigners doing business or living in Korea, it is an advantage to have some knowledge of the Korean language. Becoming fluent in Korean is a formidable task, but learning enough to communicate on a basic level is possible for someone who is prepared to undertake two or three months of daily sustained study. In business meetings, an understanding of a few Korean words and phrases can be useful when Koreans break from English to clarify a point in their own language. It is possible to follow the trend of the discussion if not the detailed content. Also, on a personal basis, Koreans greatly appreciate those who make the effort to learn. It helps to develop relationships.

HOTELS AND *YOGWANS*

Most foreigners begin their stay in Korea in one of the major hotels. The best of these rate with the best in any country in the world, with kind, cheerful and considerate service. A range of Western and Oriental cuisine is available and they boast the usual and accepted tourist facilities, bars, recreation areas and Korean barber/beauty shops. These shops give the foreigner an ideal chance to savour a Korean massage.

Any visitor who stays in Korea long will begin to travel

the country and so come face-to-face with the *Yogwan*. These are traditional Korean hotels and, although they lack some of the facilities of the main hotel chains, they offer the chance to go native for a night or two at a much lower cost. Sleeping arrangements are simple. There is a small mattress (a *Yo*) and a quilt (an *Ibul*) which are spread on the floor heated in winter by the highly effective underfloor *Ondol* heating system. Although many *Yogwans* have no restaurants, meals can be served directly in the rooms.

INVESTMENT IN KOREA

Under the Foreign Capital Inducement Law (FCIL), foreign investment is encouraged but not universally permitted for all industries. There are restricted industries such as those which receive special support from the government, or use excessive imported raw materials or are seen to produce over-extravagant consumer products. Prohibited industries include those related to public services or potentially hazardous to the environment. Any investment which may be seen as hindering development of an emerging local industry may not be welcomed. Applications are approved by the Bank of Korea if they meet a set of standard requirements but, if they fail these, are passed to the Ministry of Finance for individual review. As the years pass, there is a continuous liberalisation of foreign investment in Korea.

TYPES OF BUSINESS OPERATION

An **agency** is the simplest form of operation, but the appointed agent is not permitted to be involved in profit-earning or remitting profits out of the country. Such agencies are best used for buying goods for shipment or intelligence gathering about the local market. A **liaison office** may be opened easily as it does not conduct income-creating operations and is not, therefore, subject to corporation tax. It is required to register with the Bank of Korea in order to conduct foreign exchange transactions. It usually confines its activities to information gathering, creating business networks and straightforward buying operations.

The **branch office** is a legal entity in Korea and requires registering with a domestic court and the Bank of Korea. It can operate its business for a profit and can own assets, but it becomes taxable under Korean law and must report its existence to the tax office. There are many issues which need consideration when opening a branch office, including foreign exchange control and repatriation of earnings. When approved, the branch office must keep a legal representative in Korea, who is granted power of attorney. The **joint stock company** is the fourth class of business operation and most Korean corporations fall into this category, which is locally known as *Chusik Hoesa*. They are permitted to issue shares or bonds and at least three directors are required. A statutory auditor is elected by the shareholders and disclosure requirements are minimal. There are many conditions applied by the Ministry of Finance during their review of foreign business applications. The foreign company should provide meticulous documentation associated with the joint venture agreement and business or project description. The greater the level of planned foreign involvement, the more closely the application is likely to be examined.

LICENSING

Licensing of foreign technology is frequently used as a method of entry into Korea's markets. It is usually known as a Technical Assistance Agreement (TAA) and due care must be taken to avoid conflict with any of the prohibited or restricted industries denied to foreign investment. The technology to be licensed is also likely to be scrutinised carefully to ensure it is up-to-date and relevant to Korea's interest. Royalties for the use of good quality technology which is seen as a benefit to the economy is exempt from tax for the first five years.

INTELLECTUAL PROPERTY

Intellectual Property in the form of patents and trademarks is only protected in Korea when it is registered under the relevant local law concerning the rights of industrial ownership. In 1987, Korea signed the Universal Copyright Convention and agreed that foreign chemical and pharmaceutical products could be patented in Korea for a period of fifteen years from the date of post-acceptance publication, with a cap of 20 years from filing. It was also agreed that US product patent applications could be protected retrospectively, a point which was the cause of much consternation amongst EEC countries who accused Korea of unequal treatment. Eventually, after much debate in 1991, other countries were granted the same retrospective intellectual property rights. If resident in Korea, foreigners may register trademarks and patents in their own names.

SPORT

Koreans are a sport-loving people and have world-class teams in badminton, table tennis and archery. Perhaps their most famous sport is taekwondo, an unarmed martial art which originated in Korea and is now practised worldwide. In common with other martial arts, it is a means of training both body and mind. As in Japan, baseball is an immensely popular professional sport and is featured on local TV during the warmer months. Soccer also attracts large crowds and Korea probably have the top national side in the Far Eastern region, characterised by fast and skillful play.

Possibly the favourite sport with foreign visitors is skiing. There are a number of major ski resorts and many are within an hour or two's drive from Seoul. The season is brief, lasting from December to early March at best, and natural snow is sometimes in short supply. This is compensated by artificial snow but the slopes can be icy and very crowded at weekends. Ski resorts rent equipment and ski instruction is available. Koreans tend to ski like they drive!

Golf is popular but expensive. Many enthusiasts have to make do with the driving ranges which are a common sight around the city of Seoul. Good golf courses are available and many foreigners are invited to play by their Korean partners and colleagues. A successful round of golf can do much to cement business relationships. Tennis is another sport which has many Korean devotees and attracts a healthy following in the winter months on cold, crisp, sunny days. Many tennis courts are open to foreigners and have good quality clay surfaces.

Water sports are becoming increasingly popular as Koreans' disposable income and available leisure time rises. The waterways and lakes around the Republic attract increasing numbers of sailboats, speedboats and water-skiers. Scuba diving is available year round. Fishing is especially favoured by Korean men and freshwater, seashore and deep sea fishing can be enjoyed. Cheju and the Hallyosudo waterway, boasting clear blue waters, are reputed to be the prime spots for Korea's many angling fanatics. Last, and certainly not least, comes hiking, which is a supremely popular leisure-time activity, probably second only to drinking! On bright spring and autumn days, the mountain regions are filled with Korean alpinists, rock climbers and walkers. The local entrepreneurial economy in these tourist areas is geared up to the influx of visitors with portable shops and countless eating places on the most celebrated walking trails. Any visitor to Korea, even for a short period, is recommended to find a good solid pair of shoes or boots and join in this national obsession on a sunny weekend. It's great fun and reveals much about the nature of the people.

COMMON ABBREVIATIONS

FKI – The Federation of Korean Industries, a private organisation comprising of Korea's leading businesses and industries.

KCCI – The Korean Chamber of Commerce and Industry, a country-wide federation of leading business people, aimed at promoting business interests and developing commerce and industry.

KNTC – The Korea National Tourist Corporation, a most useful service to business visitor and tourist alike, which promotes tourism, attracts international conferences, develops potential tourist sites and provides a professional information service.

KFTA – The Korean Foreign Trade Association, which owns the Korea World Trade Centre and Korea Exhibition Centre, is a private organisation made up from licensed traders from throughout the country.

KOEX – The Korea Exhibition Centre, located in the Korea World Trade Centre, has facilities for exhibitions and trade fairs.

KOTRA – The Korean Trade Promotion Corporation, is a state operated but non-profit-making agency whose aim is to promote the Republic's international trade. It is located in the World Trade Centre.

KWTC – The Korea World Trade Centre, is the enormous fifty five floor tower which dominates the sky-line south of the River Han in Kangnam-gu. This important centre is the home of the KFTA, KOEX and KOTRA. It also provides useful information regarding local trade laws, taxation and shipping.

NATIONAL HOLIDAYS

Koreans celebrate a variety of different national holidays with the complication that both the Gregorian and Lunar calendars operate, hence some of the festivals change dates from year to year. Many are very traditional holidays where families gather for parties or outings and *Hanbok* may be worn. To maximise business during a visit it may be advisable to avoid visiting Korea during the Lunar New Year, *Chusok* and the Christmas/New Year's Day periods.

New Year's Day

The first two days of the year are family celebrations, looking forward to the year ahead. Many companies bring staff together round about this time for briefings to motivate the workforce for the challenges to come.

Lunar New Year

This is the New Year according to the Lunar Calendar and is the second most important national holiday. Called *Sol* in Korea, families follow ancient customs commemorating their ancestors and traditional games are played. It falls around the end of January.

Independence Movement Day

Korea's Independence Movement against Japanese colonial rule is remembered every year on March 1. Expect to see a lot of Korean flags flying. Ceremonies include a reading of the Korean Proclamation of Independence.

Arbor Day

This is on April 5 and is a day for planting trees, an activity which takes place nationwide as part of Korea's reforestation policy.

Children's Day

As the weather has warmed, Children's Day on May 5 is celebrated by youngsters who throng to parks and play areas.

Buddha's Birthday

A colourful and deeply traditional cultural holiday during which believers pack Buddhist temples across the nation. A huge lantern parade is held in Seoul around this time and thousands of lanterns will have appeared in temple courtyards ready to be lit on the evening of the day itself. Local temples are well worth a visit on Buddha's birthday and will yield memorable photographs. The holiday is on the eighth day of the fourth month of the lunar calendar, around May time.

Memorial Day

On June 6, those who gave their lives in battle are remembered in services held at national cemetries.

Constitution Day

The Constitution of the Republic of Korea was proclaimed on July 17, 1948 and this national holiday commemorates that important day for the country's people.

Liberation Day

Another key event still in the memories of many Koreans is the Japanese surrender on August 15, 1945 which freed the country from years of oppression. Liberation Day commemorates that surrender to the Allied army.

Chusok

The early autumn Thanksgiving Day is the most important national holiday in Korea's calendar. It is the time when Koreans visit family tombs and offer food to their ancestors. It is also a time for the visitor to avoid travelling around Korea as roads and the national transport network become clogged! *Chusok* is a major present-giving time within the business as well as the home environment and foreigners would do well to take advice from Korean colleagues as to the most suitable gifts. This joyful Thanksgiving Day falls on the fifteenth day of the eighth month of the lunar calendar, around the end of September.

National Foundation Day

This second autumn holiday is on October 3, usually very close to *Chusok* and often celebrated as a part of a longer Thanksgiving holiday, commemorates the foundation day of the very first Korean Kingdom – Ko Choson – reputedly way back in 2333 BC.

Christmas

The final national holiday is Christmas, when the Christian community enjoys its December 25 celebration. Presents are exchanged at this time, but rather less so than at the two main lunar festivals. It comes as a shock to some foreigners to be back at work on December 26.

THE KOREAN FLAG

The Korean flag dates back over one hundred years, and typically the Korean people regard it with great pride. It symbolizes the balance and harmony of opposite forces in nature, called *Um-Yang* in Korean (Yin-Yang in other parts of the Orient) and these are represented by the two parts of the centre circle. The upper red *Yang* is masculine, positive, constructive, light. The lower blue *Um* is feminine, negative, destructive, dark. The black symbols in the four corners, starting clockwise on the top left hand side, represent heaven, moon, earth and sun, or the four seasons or four cardinal points. Koreans also say that the white background means peace and the circle surrounding the *Um-Yang* signifies a unique people.

NATIONAL FLOWER

Korean people also take pride in their national flower, the Rose of Sharon (*Mugunghwa*) because it symbolises their strong but simple spirit. Perhaps the most memorable flower for most visitors to Korea, however, is the Cosmos which gives a splendid show on the roadside verges during September.

CRAFT AND CULTURE

It's difficult to avoid exposure to at least some of Korea's craft and culture. The **architecture** is of unmistakable Chinese origin but has been Koreanised and simplified with gentle curves to harmonise with the environment. Some buildings are very old and the modern reproductions are skilfully constructed to blend in with original nearby structures. Some of these buildings show **painting** techniques which date back hundreds of years. Early Korean painting showed animals such as flying horses, tigers and dragons. Developments included depiction of notable botanical species such as the plum, chrysanthemum and bamboo. The misty mountain landscapes have also featured strongly as in other Oriental countries. Window-shopping in Insa-Dong will reveal all of these plus a contemporary influence from Western art. Results can be very attractive.

Pottery possibly remains Korea's most notable contribution to the arts and perhaps the country's potters most significant achievement was the perfection of Celadon in the Koryo Dynasty. The delicate green colour is the most famous and, when applied over the inlaid decoration, gives supremely attractive pots of superb quality.

Important, but of less interest to most visitors, is the art of **calligraphy** or writing with a brush. In the past, during Choson times it flourished amongst the academic community and still has its devotees in modern Korea.

Music and Dance has always been popular amongst Koreans and they remain a very musical race. Folk music is loud, raucous and typified by the colourful Farmers' Dance, whilst Korean Court music is an absolute contrast being slow and very solemn in nature. Most of the music is composed from a five-note scale rather than the seven-note scale common in the West. To the untrained ear this means that an orchestra of traditional Korean string and wind instruments sounds out of tune! **Mask Dance Drama** has been revived in recent years and is perhaps the most popular of all Korean drama. Masks have played an important role in many cultures and in Korea, masked plays were believed to have originated thirteen hundred years ago. The art form was preserved by the common people for whom drama acted as a form of release for their frustrations against the ruling classes. Humour and satire play a major part in the stories which can often easily be followed by foreigners through the mime and antics of the players. The drama may display doubtful behaviour by the Buddhist clergy and dubious antics of the aristocracy with wives and concubines!

Finally, Korea has a distinguished tradition of being at the forefront of oriental handicrafts. This is visibly evident in the quality and workmanship of the many beautiful types of Korean chests, exquisite inlaid laquerware, mulberry paper-making and woodcarving. The visitor who buys wisely can return home with many beautiful examples of Korean arts, crafts and culture.

INTANGIBLE CULTURAL ASSETS

Korea's intense pride in heritage has encouraged the nation to nominate tangible cultural assets such as ancient buildings and artefacts. However, what makes the country very special, is their establishment of intangible cultural assets associated with art, drama, music, dance, rituals and even traditional manufacturing skills. Such desire for preservation is founded on nationalism following the attempts to destroy Korean identity under Japanese colonial rule. Even the skills of rural activities are said to need preserving and to achieve the goal, human cultural assets are appointed to nurture the intangible cultural heritage. They are experts in their particular field and pass on their knowledge and skill to willing students. This is one area where Korea should be applauded for being far-sighted for the benefit of future generations.

SERVICES

Electricity outlets of 110 and 220 volts are available but definitely worth checking before plugging in equipment.

Water quality is not up to Western European or American standards and it is inadvisable to drink unboiled tap water even in major hotels. Bottled water is freely available and is of a reliable high quality. Deliveries of larger volumes can be arranged direct to rented houses and apartments.

Car Rental is available for those brave enough to enter the fray in the streets of the major cities – although there maybe plenty of time to consult the map whilst stationary in traffic jams! Drivers must have at least one year's driving experience, be over twenty-one years of age, possess a valid passport and be in possession of an international driving licence. Chauffeur-driven cars are also available and may well be worth the extra money in saved time and frustration. The best of these professional drivers will know their way around the jams!

USEFUL ADDRESSES

Korea World Trade Centre (KWTC)
159 Samsong-dong
Kangnam-gu
Seoul
Tel: (02) 551 5114
Fax: (02) 551 5100

Korea Trade Promotion Corporation (KOTRA)
Address: As above
Tel: (02) 551 4181
Fax: (02) 551 4317

Korea Exhibition Centre (KOEX)
Address: As above
Tel: (02) 551 0114
Fax: (02) 555 7414

Korea Foreign Trade Association (KFTA)
Address: As above
Tel: (02) 551 5114
Fax: (02) 551 5100

Korea Chamber of Commerce and Industry (KCCI)
Namdaemunno 4-ga
Chung-gu
Seoul
Tel: (02) 757 0757
Fax: (02) 757 9475

Federation of Korean Industries (FKI)
28-1, Youido-dong,
Yongdungpo-gu
Seoul
Tel: (02) 780 0821
Fax: (02) 782 6425

KNTC Tourist Information Centre (Head Office)
10, Ta-dong, Chung-gu
Seoul 100-180
Tel: (02) 757 6030
Fax: (02) 757 5997

Kimpo Airport Information Centre
1st Floor, Airport Terminal Buildings 1 and 2,
Kimpo International Airport
Seoul
Tel: (02) 665 0088/0988

Kimhae Airport Information Centre
218 Taejo 2-dong, Puk-gu
Pusan
Tel: (051) 98 1100

Royal Asiatic Society
Korea Branch
CPO Box 255
Seoul
Tel: (02) 763 9483
Fax: (02) 766 3796

SUGGESTED READING

This is by no means an exhaustive list of the available literature on Korea, but it does indicate the range of topics covered and all can be recommended for a good informative read.

Republic of Korea – A Guide for Businessmen and Investors published by Samil Accounting Corporation and Coopers and Lybrand.
The Rise of the Korean Economy – Byung Nak Song published by Oxford University Press.

Insight Guides – Korea (Apa Productions, Hong Kong).

Living in Korea – published by the Seoul International Publishing Company for the American Chamber of Commerce in Korea.

Discovering Seoul – D.N. Clark and J.H. Grayson published by Seoul Computer Press for Royal Asiatic Society, Korea Branch.

Introducing Korea – edited by Peter Hyun published by the Jungwoo-sa, Seoul, Korea. (1979)

Korea's Cultural Roots – Dr Jon Carter Covell published by Hollyin International Corporation.

I Married a Korean – Agnes Davies Kim published by the John Day Company for the Royal Asiatic Society.

Korea Fantasia – Photography by John Chang McCurdy published by Seoul International Publishing House.

Korea Travel Manual – published by Korea National Tourist Corporation.

The Korean War – Max Hastings published by Michael Joseph.

A Walk through the Land of Miracles – Simon Winchester published by Grafton.

Culture Shock Korea – Sonja Vegdahl Hur and Ben Seunghwa Hur published by Times Book International.

Asia's Next Giant – Alice Amsden published by Oxford University Press.

Korea and the World Economy – Sakong Il published by Institute of International Economics.

Management Style and Practice of Korean Chaebols – S. Yoo and S. Lee published by California Management Review.

A Handbook of Korea – published by Korean Overseas Information Service.

A Letter from a Korean Village – W.J. Burns and David Kim published by Korea Save the Children, Seoul (for children).

11
Survival Guide

> The wise blames himself, a fool grumbles to friends.
>
> *Chinese proverb*

It's not unknown for visitors to Korea to undergo terminal culture shock, usually due to their own failure to comprehend the people, their traditions and their ways of doing business. Unfortunately, it's the Koreans who are often blamed for communication breakdown whilst frustrated Westerners return muttering about Oriental unwillingness to negotiate on reasonable terms. This final chapter summarises the important points presented through earlier pages in the book, to help emphasise the factors which will make business easier and any stay in Korea, short or long, more enjoyable and less stressful.

Korea itself is a country undergoing immense internal stress as a result of its rapid economic development, but of all the Eastern Asian emerging economies, it is probably the one best placed to follow Japan and join the major league of the world's most successful industrialised nations. Korea has much to offer, is keen to internationalise, and increasingly wishes to contribute towards open trade by progressively withdrawing protectionist barriers.

COUNTRY SKETCH

Geographical Position

- At an Asian cross-roads between China, Russia, Mongolia and Japan.

Climate

- Truly the 'Land of Four Seasons' which makes it a comfortable place in which to live and work.

Chinese Influence

- Much of the culture originated in China although it has been developed and Koreanised.

Population

- A distinct group, who migrated many centuries ago from Mongolia. There are over 43 million in South Korea, one of the most densely populated countries on Earth.

Topography

- Korea is mountainous, with most of the staple rice-crop grown in the flatter areas in the West.

History

- Turbulent, punctuated by frequent invasions and occupation by neighbouring countries. This has resulted in mistrust of foreigners and fear of domination by others.

North Korea

- Begins at the 38th Parallel. Over twenty million North Koreans live in a specialist Communist regime under the dictator Kim Il-Sung. It is a poor and isolated country.

Religion

- Buddhism claims more followers than any other religion. However, there are many Christians and Taoism and Shamanism also have their devotees. All these are overlaid by Confucian principles.

FACTORS AFFECTING ECONOMIC DEVELOPMENT

Will to Succeed

- One of Korea's most notable strengths is the people's positive orientation to succeed, as evidenced by their hosting of the 1988 Olympic Games.

Government

- Successive governments have been far-sighted in planning economic development and channelling funds to growth and export industries encouraging the people to work hard for a better future.

Protectionism

- Protectionist barriers were originally built around strategic industries. Companies trading with or operating in Korea still encounter difficulties which stem from central government protectionist involvement and variable bureaucratic interpretation of guidelines. However, the barriers are steadily being dismantled.

Internationalisation

- The country has chosen to internationalise as rapidly as possible, encouraging inward technology transfer and outward investment by the *Chaebol*. However, until recently, few Koreans had travelled abroad and their perception of the world outside is limited.

Change in Industrial Structure

- Korea's early growth centred around heavy engineering, construction projects, ship-building and textiles. The economy has progressed steadily towards higher technology products with a fast growing automotive, electronic and semiconductor powerbase. Much of the technology is still imported from Japan.

Political Scene

- The transfer of presidential power from Chun Doo-Hwan to Roh Tae-Woo in 1987 was the first peaceful one in Korea's modern history. The hastening of the democratisation process which followed and changing political spectrum elsewhere in the world, has opened up important new markets in China and Russia. Kim Young-Sam's presidential term will see continuation and probably acceleration of the activity.

Reunification

- Will they, won't they? North Korea becomes increasingly isolated as Communism yields around the world. However, Kim Il-Sung and his son Kim Jong-Il still retain a firm hold. Moves toward reunification continue slowly but hit frequent stumbling blocks. South Koreans have watched the German model nervously.

DISTINCTLY KOREAN

Nationalism

- Koreans are very nationalistic and greatly appreciate the beauty and special features of their own country. This is a trait strengthened by years of domination, colonial rule and exploitation by outsiders.

Confucianism

- This has been the main influence on the Korean way of life for hundreds of years and has principles of loyalty, trust, a well-ordered social structure and harmony in personal and business relationships.

Etiquette

- Koreans are well-mannered people, courteous and with strict codes of etiquette. Visitors are treated formally and pleasantly, the latter accentuated by gestures designed to create a good mood and smooth the path of potential relationships. It is called *Kibun*.

Personal Touch

- Interaction between Koreans is a very personal affair, bolstered by networks of contacts and a marked level of honour and trust. Foreigners must adapt to the system.

'Face'

- 'Face' refers to a person's reputation, position in business or society and the overall image to others. In Korea, as in most Asian countries, it is fiercely protected and a threat to 'face' can cause severe problems.

Lack of Creativity

- Passion for education is a Confucian principle and has led to a high literacy rate in Korea. However, Koreans are not the most creative people, at least partly due to their 'learning by rote' school system.

Unique Identity

- Although many aspects of Korean culture arrived from China and moved on to Japan, the Koreans are proud of a unique identity. They are less restrained than the Japanese and visitors invariably receive a favourable initial impression.

CHARACTER OF THE PEOPLE

Gregarious

- Koreans are gregarious, fun-loving people, who are devoted to their families and love children. They dress well and are cultivated, appreciating Western art and music.

Hard Workers

- The Korean working week is amongst the longest in the world. Personal loyalties within the office means they will frequently work well into the evening. However, they are not always too productive with their efforts.

Stubborn

- They are stubborn and extraordinarily patient. As the people are always courteous as well, this can be very frustrating to a hot-headed visitor who wants quick results!

Ceremonial

- Many traditional rituals are still practised passionately, including 100th day celebrations for babies and splendid sixtieth year birthday parties for the elder generation. Many Koreans wear *Hanbok* national dress on certain public holidays.

Women

- The fair sex have traditionally played a subservient role in society, and although changing slowly, it is still prevalent in social and office life.

Consumer Behaviour

- Most Koreans consider themselves middle-class and their behaviour patterns operate accordingly. They like shopping at department stores and increasingly enjoy leisure and sporting pursuits as their disposable income grows.

Cultural Skills

- The nation encourages continuation of ancient artistic skills, as evidenced by the fine quality of ceramic ware, painting and lacquerware. There is much to enjoy.

Cuisine

- Korean food is an essential part of the character of the people. It's nutritious, low in calories, fiery to taste, always taken with rice and has peppers and garlic as important ingredients.

BUSINESS CULTURE

Introduction

- Try and organise a formal introduction to future colleagues and business associates. It is considered polite. If you are not known beforehand, try and use an intermediary to make the introduction.

Business Card

- Never be without one! It should give your name, company and title in your own language and Korean. Business card exchange is a formal affair made at time of introduction and hand-shake.

Develop Relationships

- The formal written word is less important in Korea than the development and subsequent fostering of close and good personal relationships. Time spent on this and getting to know your counterpart is never wasted and benefits will follow later.

Patience

- This is a gift from heaven for those who work in Korea and must be featured as a part of a foreigner's personal development plan. Always be prepared to delay sensitive issues to another meeting and never push too hard.

Communicate

- Concisely – English is the most common foreign business language in the country and Koreans' comprehension is not as good as one immediately thinks. One of the most common traps for the unwary visitor is to believe that everything has been understood. It frequently hasn't. Always repeat key points, try giving a written brief beforehand and exchange notes after a meeting.

Entertain

- Entertainment is a significant part of business etiquette. Eat, drink and be merry. Explore Korean cuisine, sing lustily when requested and be prepared to 'let your hair down'. Enjoy it and it will pay dividends.

Remember *Kibun*

- Create good feelings by being positive (not always easy!), congratulating colleagues on successful achievements. Spend time praising not criticising.

Emotion

- Korea is an emotional place. Western logic doesn't always apply, so let emotion and abstract, subjective thoughts pass through the mind if you are to understand some of the surprising decisions and activities that abound.

IN A KOREAN COMPANY

Status

- Status in the company is important, is visible within the office and promotion may depend upon age not just ability. The hierarchy is likely to be more rigidly structured than in a Western company.

Social Structure

- Groups and friendships in the organisation may depend upon university affiliations, military acquaintances or even birthplace. Foreigners may need to observe carefully to spot the really influential staff members and groupings.

Recruitment and Dismissal

- As a result of status and social structure, matters of recruitment and dismissal need careful handling. The most suitable staff are likely to be found using networks of personal contacts. Go Korean not Western-style in these matters.

Unions

- The labour union movement is still rather fragmented but can wield embarrassing short term difficulties in foreign Joint Ventures. Korean workers are enjoying a larger slice of the 'cake' and can behave nationalistically to achieve their ends.

Secretary

- A good secretary is a valuable asset to a foreigner in Korea and can help overcome the cultural barrier. Used wisely, she can be a source of priceless information about Office politics and everyday events in the country.

Working Hours

- Long! This exacerbates the tiredness and stress factors of working in Korea. Foreigners need to make their own judgement as to what is best but as Westerners are more productive from their daily chores, it may be best to enjoy a relaxing 'earlier' night from time to time.

Motivating Staff

- Delegate wisely and with guidance. Be diplomatic and communicate with great care. Entertain when necessary, encourage the group spirit and staff training. Remember Confucius!

CONFLICT

Understand the Korean Viewpoint

- Despite yearning for internationalisation Koreans want to adopt an independent, self-reliant approach to business, free of domination by foreigners. They are sensitive about potentially losing control.

Conflict Sources

- Many are related to differing styles of management and culture, even the global strategy of a multinational company. Management control in a joint venture may be challenged, so may transfer pricing or personnel policies. Virtually anything may become a friction point if handled badly.

Conflict Prevention

- Full marks to anyone who can truly prevent it. Patience helps enormously, and lines of communication must be kept open at all times. Develop and maintain sincere relationships and keep records of all dialogue and meetings to avoid future misunderstandings.

Conflict Resolution

- Pay attention to the 'Korean Way' and work on *Kibun*. Be patient, diplomatic and prepare to yield some ground in negotiations. Applying Western logic may be counter-productive and losing one's temper is not likely to help. If conflict is severe, use a mediator.

LIVING IN KOREA

Hotels

- The major hotels are excellent and can make a comfortable, enjoyable start to a posting in Korea.

Housing

- Rental of houses and apartments is expensive and maybe one year or more rental charge could be required up front. Bear in mind workplace, shops, social life and schooling before choosing accommodation. A residence in the wrong place can mean hours sitting in horrendous traffic jams.

Western-Style Goods

- These become increasingly available and foreigners should not need to go without much. Fresh produce is available, supermarkets are reasonable quality and clothes shopping is an absolute delight.

Transport

- Driving a car requires nerve and an ability to be defensive behind the wheel. Foreigners who need to travel even short distances frequently are recommended to employ a driver. Taxis are useful, the Subway in Seoul convenient, National Rail network fast and comfortable, and domestic air travel effective.

Leisure

- In Seoul, social activities for expatriates tend to revolve around the Seoul Club. Sporting enthusiasts should note that skiing in winter and tennis all the year round are popular. Badminton and table tennis are played to world-class standards by Koreans. Hiking is immensely popular.

Tourism

- There are tremendous opportunities to explore near and far in Korea, enjoy the beautiful countryside and admire the cultural past. Mountain scenery is splendid everywhere, notably at Soraksan National Park. Want to spend a relaxing weekend? Try Cheju Island, easily accessible by air.

Children

- Foreign schools are generally regarded as very good. Recommended visits for children are Lotte World, Seoul Grand Park and Yongin Farmland. If housebound, then plenty of suitable videos can be hired cheaply.

Index

Adaptability, Korean 41
Adversity 101
Advertising 106
Agency 141
Altaic 39
American Embassy 118
American *see* USA
Anglican Cathedral 118
Antiques 118, 124
Arbor Day 147
Architecture 150
Armistice 22
ASEAN 62–3
Asian Games 3

Benefits 95–6
Bulgogi 51
Birth 44
Books *see* Reading list
Bowing 46
Branch office 142
British Embassy 118
Buddha's birthday 118, 147
Buddhism 5, 12, 118
Buses 117
Business, card 69–70, 164
Business, etiquette 55–8

Calligraphy 150
Car Rental 152
Catholic Cathedral 119
Celadon 13, 127, 150
Central Korea 130
Ceremony, family 43–5
Chaebol 26, 30, 63–6, 88, 92, 94, 102

Chang Myon 23
Changdok Palace 120
Changgyong Palace 120
Cheju Island 45, 132–4, 144
Children's Day 147
China 9, 11, 12, 17, 22, 62–3, 140, 158
Chindo Island 132
Chiri-san National Park 132
Chogori 53
Chogye-sa Temple 118
Choi Kyu-Itah 25
Chondung-sa Temple 129
Chongmyo, Shrine 120
Chop 94–5
Choson, Kingdom 14–16
Christianity 6
Chun Doo-Hwan, President 25
Chunchon Lake 127
Chung Ju-Yung 64
Chungju Reservoir 130
Chungmun Resort 133
Chusok 54, 68, 148
Clan 10, 45, 68, 79
Climate 116, 158
Commitment 55–6
Communication 75–7, 96, 108, 136, 165
Compromise 111
Concensus 59
Confidentiality 85–6, 112
Conflict, prevention 46, 107, 168
Conflict, resolution 109–13, 168

171

Conflict, sources   104–7, 167
Confucian, Academy   43, 120
Confucianism   4, 5, 14–15, 41–3, 67–8, 74, 91, 94, 96, 161
Confucius   43, 68, 109
Constitution   24, 49, 135
Constitution Day   148
Consultant   *see* Intermediary
Contract   71, 80, 107–8
Copyright   86, 143
Cotton   53
Counterfeit goods   124
Cultural assets   151–2
Cultural boundaries   81
Culture   150–1, 163
Currency   138
Custom Tailor   123

Daehan Building   121
Daewoo   56, 65
Decision, making   86–7
Delegation   97
Demilitarised Zone (DMZ)   22, 116, 128
Democracy   25
Democratic Republican Party   24
Dismissal   90–91, 166
Downtown, Seoul 118–19
Dragon Valley   *see* Yongpyeong
Dragons   35

Eastern Korea   129–30
Eastern Sea   9, 67
Economic Planning Board   36–7
Economic Plans   33–6
Economy   29–38, 159–61
Education, Korean   88

Electricity   152
Engineering maintenance   105
Entertainment   71–3, 78, 103, 165
Entry, points   136
Entry, requirements   137
Etiquette   46–7, 82, 161
Etiquette, elements   69–75
European Community   38
Exchange rate   138
Export   30–3

Face   47–8, 87, 90, 96, 162
Female   *see* women
Finance   32, 103
Fishing   127, 144
FKI   145, 153
Flag, Korean   149
Food, Korean   50–2, 122, 126
Freedom Bridge   128
Freedom House   128

Gambling   125
General trading companies   32, 35
Genghis Khan   13
Geography   115–17, 158
Gifts   73
Ginseng   52–3, 129
Goldstar   65
Golf   109, 144
Gospel Central Church   121
Government decisions   87
Group spirit   96

Haein-sa Temple   13, 132
Halla-san Mountain   133
Hallyosudo Waterway   132, 144
Hamel, Hendrik   16

Index

Han, River 3, 117, 121, 128
Hanbok 43, 53–4, 72, 146
Hangul 5, 14, 140
Harmony 42, 46, 74–5
Health care 139
Hemp 53
Hermit, Kingdom 5, 15
Hideyoshi, Togotomi 15
Hiking 109, 127, 144–5
Hirobumi, Ito 18
Homes, Korean 48–9
Hotels 140–1, 168
Housing 138, 168
Humility 57
Hwangap 43
Hyangwon Pavilion 120
Hyundai 29, 64

Ichon 127
IMAX Theatre 121
Imjin, River 128
Inchon 21
Independence Hall 130
Independence Movement Day 147
Insa-dong 118, 124
Intellectual property 143
Intermediary 69, 78, 102, 112–13
Investment 38, 141
Itaewon 123, 125

Japan 12, 15, 16, 17, 29, 36, 58–62, 67
Japan, colonial rule 18–19, 151
Joint stock company 142
Joint venture 91–2, 102

Kaesong 12, 13
Kalbi 51

Kanghwa Island 10, 13, 53, 128–9
Karaoke 125
KCCI 145, 153
KFTA 145, 153
Kibun 46–7, 73, 78, 165
Kim Dae-Jung 24
Kim Il-Sung 20, 24, 160
Kim Jae-Kyu 24
Kim Jong-Il 160
Kim Woo-Choong 56, 65
Kim Young-sam, President 26–7
Kimchi 50–1, 72
Kimhae Airport, telephone 154
Kimjang 50
Kimpo Airport 3, 136
Kimpo Airport, telephone 154
Kisaeng, hostess 72
KNTC 145, 154
Ko-Choson 11
KOEX 146, 153
Koguryo Kingdom 11
Kojong, King 13, 16
Korea House 122
Korean, executives 93–5, 98–9
Korean, folk village 44, 126
Korean, language 76, 140
Korean, society 80
Korean, viewpoint 79–80, 167
Korean, war 21–3, 121, 128, 131
Koryo dynasty 12–13
KOTRA 146, 153
Kujolpan 51
Kwanak-san Mountain 128
KWTC 146, 153

Kyongbok Palace 119–20
Kyongju 11, 131
Kyongju National
    Museum 131

Liaison Office 142
Liberal, Party 23
Liberation Day 148
Licensing 142–3
Lifestyle, Korean 48–50
Lotte Store 107, 119
Lotte World 122
Loyalty 41, 59

MacArthur, Douglas 21–2
Maeuntang 51
Makkoli 125
Management, style 55–66
Management, control 105
Management, of change 109
Manchuria 9, 11, 19
Mani-san Mountain 10, 129
March 1 Movement 18
Marketing 106, 107
Markets 123–4
Marriage 44–5
Mary's Alley *see* Insa-dong
Mask dance drama 151
Mediator *see* Intermediary
Memorial Day 148
Military Armistice
    Commission 22–3
Min, Queen 17
Ming, Dynasty 13
Ministry of Trade and
    Industry 32
Mongolia 39
Mongols 13, 39
Motivation, staff 95–8, 167
Music 122, 125–6, 150–1
Myong-dong 118–19, 124

Nam-san Mountain 117, 122
Nam-san Tower 122
Namdaemun 123–4
Names, Korean 45–6
Namhansansong
    Fortress 128
Namisom 127
National Assembly 121, 135
National Flower 149–50
National Foundation
    Day 10, 148–9
National holidays 146–9
National Museum 118
Negotiation 77–8
New Democratic Party 24
Newly Industrialised
    Country (NIC) 35
Newspapers 139
Night life 125–6
North Korea 11, 20, 21–3,
    24, 26, 68, 159

Odae-san National Park 130
Olympic Complex 121
Olympic Stadium 3, 121
Ondol 11, 48–9
Organisation 106

Paekche Kingdom 11
Painting 124, 150
Palaces, Seoul 119–20
Panmunjon 23, 128
Park Chung-Hee,
    President 24, 30, 32
Patent 86, 143
Patience 40, 74, 97, 107, 164
Payments 87–8, 94
Personal, touch 73, 161
Pharmacies 139
Piwon 120
Policies 107

Pomun Lake Resort 131
Popchu-sa Temple 130
Pop-ju 51, 72
Population 116, 136
Pottery see Celadon
President 135
Productivity 85
Pukan-san Mountain 128
Pukansansong Fortress 128
Pulguk-sa Temple 12, 131
Pusan 21, 130, 131, 136
Pyongyang 10, 16

Quality, control 105

Rangoon 26
Reading list 154–5
Records 108
Recruitment 89–90
Relationship, building 70–1, 164
Relationship, Confucian 41–2
Relationship, personal 46, 79, 109
Rice 52
Roh Tae-Woo, President 25–6
Royal Asiatic Society (RAS) 134, 154
Russia 17, 19–20

Salary 95, 106
Samsung 29, 64, 65
Schools 138
Secret Garden see Piwon
Secretary 83, 84, 90, 166
Sejong Cultural Centre 118
Sejong, King 14, 119
Sejong-no 15, 118
Seniority 57–8

Seoul 20, 21, 50, 117–26, 137
Seoul, Club 90
Seoul, Grand Park 126
Shamanism 10
Shopping 123–4
Silk 53
Silla, Kingdom 4, 11–12
Singing 72
Skiing 144
Sogni-san National Park 130
So-ju 61, 72, 125
Sokkuram Hermitage 12, 131
Sorak-san National Park 127, 129
South East Korea 130–2
South West Korea 132
Soyang, Lake 127
Sport 143–5
Status 82–4, 166
Stock Exchange 50, 121
Stubbornness, Korean 40, 163
Subway 117
Sung, Dynasty 13
Sunjong, King 120
Supermarkets 169
Syngman Rhee, President 20, 22, 23

Taedong, River 16
Taekwondo 4, 143
Taiwan 58–62
Tangun 10, 129
Taoism 40
Taxis 117
Technology, transfer 38, 78, 86
Tennis 109, 144
Theatre restaurants 125
Thirty Eighth Parallel 19, 22
Titles 46

Tobong-san Mountain   128
Toksu Palace   119
Tolharubang Statues   133
Tongdaemun   124
Tours   117
Trademark   143
Training   97–8
Trains   117
Travel   116–17
Treaty, of Portsmouth   17
Tripitaka Koreana   13, 132
Truman, President
Tumuli Park   131
Turtle, ship   15

UN   20, 21–3, 131
Unions   92–3, 166
University   83, 88
USA   19–20, 62–3

Visas   137

Wang Kon   12
War Museum   121
Water   152

Wedding   44–5
Wedding, halls   44
Western, logic   46, 110
Whisky   73
Women, employees   91–2
Women, role   48–50, 163
Working hours   84, 167

Yalu, River   22
Yangban   15, 74
Yellow Sea   9, 21
Yi Song-Gye   13
Yi Sung-Man   *see* Syngman Rhee
Yi, dynasty   14–16, 119, 120
Yi, Sun-shin   15, 118, 132
Yogwan   140–1
Yoido Island   2, 120–1
Yoido, Plaza   121
Yong-dong   125
Yongdong Expressway   129, 130
Yongin Farmland   126
Yongpyeong Ski Resort   130
Yu-gyo   *see* Confucianism